The Not Good Enough Mother

SHARON LAMB

Beacon Press
BOSTON

BEACON PRESS
Boston, Massachusetts
www.beacon.org

Beacon Press books
are published under the auspices of
the Unitarian Universalist Association of Congregations.

22 21 20 19   8 7 6 5 4 3 2 1

This book is printed on acid-free paper that meets the uncoated paper
ANSI/NISO specifications for permanence as revised in 1992.

Text design and composition by Kim Arney

Many names and identifying characteristics of people mentioned in
this work have been changed to protect their identities. As is recommended
in writing about clients, individuals and their life histories are
composites of several individual and life histories.

Library of Congress Cataloging-in-Publication Data

Names: Lamb, Sharon, author.
Title: The not good enough mother / Sharon Lamb.
Description: Boston : Beacon Press, 2019.
Identifiers: LCCN 2018043299 (print) | LCCN 2018053087 (ebook) |
ISBN 9780807082478 (ebook) | ISBN 9780807082461 (hardback)
Subjects: LCSH: Parenting. | Child rearing. | Mother and child. | BISAC:
FAMILY & RELATIONSHIPS / Parenting / Motherhood. |
BIOGRAPHY & AUTOBIOGRAPHY / Social Scientists &
Psychologists. | PSYCHOLOGY / Psychopathology / Addiction.
Classification: LCC HQ769 (ebook) | LCC HQ769 .L1776 2019 (print) |
DDC 306.874—dc23
LC record available at https://lccn.loc.gov/2018043299

For Paul
For Willy
For Julian

And for all mothers and othermothers.
We want to give our children the world.
We end up giving them ourselves and hope that that's good enough.

Contents

PROLOGUE

"MAMA, MAMA, MAMA, MAMA, MAMA, MAMA." Her crying filled the hot car. It had been sitting in the Vermont summer sun for an hour before I took off down the country road, kicking up a fog of dust behind me. Strapped in a car seat between her older sister and older brother, Krystle wailed for the mother we were driving away from inside the battered white house that I could still see in the rearview mirror. A house with no electricity, no running water, no toys, no place to play. I didn't really believe it was their mother's house. I was pretty sure it was a place she had borrowed for what had been the all-important home observation.

Krystle's crying grew in intensity. I checked the mirror again and saw that her towheaded older sister and brother were trying not to cry. I sped up, but then the wails started. Although five and seven years old, the siblings tapped into a very early memory of what it meant to howl like a baby, with a full, open-throated cry. Not the healthy cry that demands what it wants when it wants it, but the bereft moan of helplessness. Hopelessness. *Mama, Mama, Mama.* Three children in agony, finding their rhythm and maybe some comfort in their chorus.

"We'll be at your daddy's soon," I said. "I know. I know, you miss your mommy." I couldn't offer comfort by telling the children that they'd see their mother again. I didn't know that they would. After this visit, and for a variety of other reasons, I was leaning away from recommending that they be returned to her.

I take children away from their parents. Sometimes permanently.

1

Perhaps I'm being too dramatic when I assume such full responsibility. Yet when I complete an evaluation and write a report recommending the termination of parental rights, supporting a "TPR," the judge frequently takes my advice. Both the judicial and social service systems crank into gear when a child has been abused or neglected, and there are many individuals who monitor parents' progress and failures. But in the end, I retain the feeling—and maybe that's what's important here, my feeling—that the responsibility is all on me. And I feel heartless.

There are others. There are social workers from the Department of Children and Families, DCF in Vermont, who document the failure of parents to comply with requests to make their home safer or attend therapy or give up drugs. I use their reports. Lawyers representing the state, the parents, and even the child give me perspectives from all sides and later, in court, make arguments ranging from cogent to ridiculous about my evaluation and written report. Other witnesses in court bring in facts on what they have observed: the domestic argument overheard through the walls or a toddler unsupervised playing in the garbage out back behind her house or the child found alone at home with nothing in the cabinets to eat. Their contributions are very important, but the expert is crucial. When I bring in the purportedly scientific facts and theories from the field of psychology and child development, basic stuff I teach my students who are training to be counselors or psychologists, I draw from the empirical literature. I explain attachment categorizations and how these help us to understand this particular little girl's behavior or that particular boy's relationship with his mother. I give my opinion to judges who lean forward and show respect. So maybe I am to blame, or more accurately, responsible for the outcome.

What's there is there, though, sometimes leaving little to interpretation. I try to report on what's there between a mother and a child, between the parents I evaluate and their children. I do this primarily through observations. But I use other pieces of evidence as well, before making my recommendations. When I perform an evaluation, I read through a pile of previously written reports, including ones by other psychologists. There can be many reports before mine. Sometimes a different psychologist provides an evaluation, one to determine the mental health of each parent, another to evaluate the developmental trauma of a child, another, typically from a school psychologist, to provide the academic, social, and psychological work-up. There are also DCF case plans and case dispositions, formal reports that monitor progress. There are documents that show the merit of removing a child via a CHINS, a Child in Need of Services order. There are copious handwritten notes of visit supervisors. There are social worker affidavits, which are long lists of purported facts written in such simple nondescriptive language that they beg to be prioritized as truth over the complex narratives in case plans. There are police affidavits. The facts are formally dressed with times and dates as if to say that numbers remembered and inserted are truer than the noting of a comforting hand on the child's shoulder or the gaze of the child towards his mother. They go like this: Jane Doe was arrested at 10:38 p.m. on August 4, 2001, for attempting to rob a 7-Eleven with a .44 Magnum revolver having left the Lapp Center at 5:45 p.m. taking the #33 bus. There are also written documents of phone conversations with therapists, physicians, pediatricians, teachers, superintendents, family interventionists, substance abuse counselors, probation officers, parenting program teachers, AA sponsors, coworkers, neighbors, and family members. There are personality tests that I have given, scored, and interpreted, including the controversial Rorschach, the ink-blot test, which I have come to rely on to tell me about things I can't determine from the 567 True/False items pushed and shaped into diagnoses in the commonly used personality test, the MMPI-2.

There are also notes from interviews. I play with children in the sandbox in my office as part of the child interview, noting the child who comes into my office fascinated by the wealth of toys, as well as the child who finds nothing suitable to play with: "Everything's broken here." In interviews with parents, I take their histories, gaining their trust, momentarily empathizing with their mostly unfortunate lives, damaging relationships, and generational problems that go so far back as to make me feel that there was never any hope for this family.

Observations, though, are key. I enter the houses of parents, both foster parents and biological parents, and sit in a corner taking notes. "Don't mind me," I say. The adults are gracious. They offer me coffee or tea and sometimes even dinner. They are wary and welcoming. I've heard their stories earlier in my office and have kind words for them, and so we have forged some kind of tentative bond. I am a kind person, someone recently told me, after I had said to this person that I was often taken as abrupt and irritable. I may not be kind, but I am definitely kindest in my therapy office, where I become wrapped up in the mothers' childhoods and histories of mistreatment. Sitting across from me, they are children again, who want to be heard and have a mother mirror their worth. When they are no longer in my office, when I go to their homes, where they must be parents and judged, the bond that began in my office dissolves. It is my job then and there to watch the way the mothers behave with their children, the way they try to act natural in an unnatural context and attempt to perform a version of good enough mothering for me.

I watch, sometimes sitting on the floor, computer on my lap, for signs of attachment, for praise, for affection, for authentic connections, joint attention, a certain look, as well as for missed signals, sarcasm, lack of empathy, mockery (so alarming when it occurs), and detachment. I hold back when a child comes up to me to play after a parent has failed to notice what she wanted—some indirect request to "look at me," "join me," "admire me." I carefully document when the child begins to look for my acknowledgement over her parent's as she plays.

Most of all, I sit in judgment.

Judging makes me feel powerful and knowledgeable, but also protective. A little bit in love with the children I'm observing, I want to gather them close at the end of the visit to hug them or sometimes to simply end a session by joining them in the delicious intimacy of their fantasy play.

But sometimes I sit in judgment of myself. Who am I to make these determinations? I begin to compare myself to the mother I'm watching, finding myself lacking and not good enough. All the empathy I can extend to others in my office, the critique of the construction of mothering in our culture that I teach to my Human Development students, the anthropological literature on different forms of mothering that I am well aware of, all of it does me no good. I am a wreck and lost in a kind of hazy confusion that comes when one allows oneself to loosen the boundaries between professional and client, good mother and bad.

The psychoanalyst D. W. Winnicott suggested that there are no good mothers, only good enough mothers. My friends tell me that I shouldn't judge my parenting by the way my kids have turned out and that, actually, they're not through developing and incidentally are lovely people. They say I must remember that my husband had a hand in raising them too, and that their peers have had an influence. My therapist tells me to stop my black-and-white thinking. My Al-Anon parents' group says, "Don't compare your insides with other people's outsides." Helpful, but not helpful enough to allay the particular kind of anxiety that modern mothering produces when one's children turn out to have problems.

Good enough mothering is obviously what that eponymous Tiger mom in *The Battle Hymn of the Tiger Mother* accomplished, even though she ripped up one of her daughter's handmade Mother's Day cards because the art was sloppy, an act that could have cost another mother access to her child if I'd been in the corner of the room observing. Her children grew up to play orchestra instruments, probably beautifully, and attended prestigious colleges. They look happy in their photos. How did that good enough mother get away with such destructive acts, even working as she did, full time as a lawyer, and still produce what I imagine to be a cohesive and successful family?

When I go to that place of "what I did wrong" and think about my job, my situation as a "working mother," the one whom the media perennially suggests neglects her children, I need to remind myself

I had summers off and the flexible schedule of an academic. Surely that's a schedule more conducive to good parenting than a lawyer's? But there you have it. The Tiger mom's children are high-achieving young women who play orchestra instruments and attend prestigious colleges and look happy in their photos. My children play instruments, beautifully too, but haven't played them for a while and are leading the lives of low-income individuals scraping by, the kinds of individuals in families that DCF keeps an eye on, the kind I judge.

PART I

Assessment

1. INFORMED CONSENT

There is a moment in my interviews of the mothers when I begin to turn on them. Typically, I am fully absorbed in their life histories, narratives that often contain multiple tragedies, from neglect to rape: the mother whose own mother, when drunk, beat her and all her siblings with a belt; the mother whose own mother didn't like her and told her so often, those words causing a searing pain whenever they're remembered; the one whose mother left her with an alcoholic step-dad and his alcoholic new wife to clean up their vomit and empty bottles in the morning before school; the one whose mother had her daughter, at thirteen years old, share a room with someone else's children, including an eighteen-year-old boy who raped her; or the one whose mother allowed her boyfriend to molest her daughter for drugs.

I am surprised that these mothers of the mothers I see have stayed so vividly in my imagination, as I've only heard about them through their daughters' reports. But like witches in fairy tales, the mothers of the mothers remain vibrant, powerful, and wicked. The mothers in the room with me are much more complicated.

When I listen to the mothers who are in the room with me, I listen intensely, writing at the same time, filling up pages with their history. They are free to talk as little or as long as they like. So many, when telling their stories, become sad or agitated or angry or all three. They perceive me as nice, maybe just for listening. And I really do feel kind towards them, because in their stories, each is both a daughter and a fellow traveler carrying that burden of motherhood.

Each mother has filled out what is called an informed consent form. This form protects me and, supposedly, it also protects them. It's meant to insure that before speaking to me, they know that whatever they say will not be kept totally confidential. I will write what they say into a report. I will share the report with their lawyer, or with the Department of Children and Families, or with the court if called upon to testify. And these people may give others this report too.

Most sign without thinking. Some ask a question or two about whether they'll get a copy of the report or what kinds of tests I'll administer, not because they have looked up these tests online but rather, like all the applicants to the academic program I run, who hate the GREs, these people also hate being tested. Once someone called her lawyer and asked if she should sign it. Occasionally, one will say that she will sign because she has no choice but to sign, that DCF has told her she has to participate in the evaluation. Ethically, I don't know what to say to this, so I ask, "Given the circumstances, are you freely agreeing to participate?" We sit there for a moment, neither of us moving. When it begins to look to her as if I won't go on without her consent, she begrudgingly says yes.

The fact is, I'm stuck. DCF has, in effect, coerced these women into the evaluation by threatening to remove their children or arguing it is necessary because the evaluation may help DCF understand next steps to take. Is it a coerced signature even if I'm not the one doing the coercing? I might probe some more before carrying on. I might even ask, "Do you want to call your lawyer and see if this is in your best interest?" I don't really expect them to say yes. While I'm covering myself, I'm also pointing out that they may have more choice than they believe they have. But probably not.

They soon forget their distrust and feelings of helplessness and talk to me. I'm interested. I put myself in the middle of their lives as if I'm a college student again reading a novel about the tragic and doomed life of a feisty heroine. Their lives are dramatic. The empathic experience isn't one of observing from the outside but more like living that experience as the mother retells it. Lives, like novels, make sense. They have coherence. I want to know if there's been bad fortune or evil trickery or love. I want to know how they understand what was done to them and what they did.

Is my empathy strategic? Calculated? No. Even if it works to relax the women I interview and help them let their guard down, it is real. And maybe because it is real, it leads them to say things that can or will change everything. Sometimes this is a single statement. I'm following someone through the events of her life, caring about her suffering, and she is talking about problems with her husband's daughter who has come to live with them and says, "That girl is pure evil." I ask how old the girl is, the girl who is "pure evil," and she tells me ten. Surely she doesn't mean what she says. I test this by offering the point of view of this ten-year-old: "So her mother abandoned her and she has been dropped into your household with a father she barely knows?" The mother answers, "Yes, but . . . ," and tells me the girl came at her with a knife in the kitchen. In her version of the story, they were arguing over which knife to use cutting tomatoes and the girl just "came at her": "That girl is evil." I know that "arguing" is not the full story. At this point I have less empathy for the woman who had to take in her husband's troubled daughter from another marriage, who was left to deal with the wreckage as her husband was out working, who had to take all the mother-hatred and ambivalence that this ten-year-old had to offer. I could have focused on all that, but at this point I am focused on the girl. Ten years old. She got stuck living with this woman who not only won't mother her but thinks she is evil and surely conveys this to the girl. My empathy has run out.

2. A MOTHER

It has been over a week since I submitted my report on the placement of Tessa and already the bright memory of her mother, Jane, is diminishing. What remains is Jane on paper. Jane on paper did not look very good as a mother. She had been addicted to opiates for almost six years and had lost two previous children to DCF because of her addiction. Tessa was her third child. Homelessness and a failure to comply with DCF requests were a part of those decisions, but these come with the addiction. She had refused to attend therapy or go into treatment for her addiction. And that is never a good sign.

When Jane became pregnant with Tessa, and knowing that DCF would take Tessa at birth, she left the state with a girlfriend, driving to a state in the Midwest where she had family, to give birth to Tessa there in hopes of keeping her. The Vermont DCF, however, was alerted that she had left and found her somehow in an Ohio hospital, a social worker arriving with paper in hand to make an official claim on the infant. The DCF worker informed Jane that Tessa would be placed in foster care back in Vermont, with her one-year-old sister and three-year-old brother, who had been adopted by the same foster mother. Jane left the hospital, before little blue-eyed Tessa, a soon-to-be pink and white baby, had completed her round of treatment for jaundice and was safe to go. Jane just left, and nobody knew where she went. Reemerging in Vermont two weeks later, she entered the DCF offices and asked for help. She didn't know what to do to get Tessa back and had realized it was best to turn to DCF and let them help her. But on paper, how did this two-week break look? It looked like she abandoned her child.

On the other hand, it is promising when a child is an infant and a mother asks for help. It is DCF's job to work towards reunification of a family until there is no longer any hope for reunification or until the child has been in custody too long. Her DCF worker found a place that would take Jane and Tessa together: the Lapp Center for substance-abusing mothers and their infants. This home permits children to be with their mothers in a supervised environment while their mothers fight their cravings and learn parenting skills. Tessa and Jane spent five nights together before Jane's urinalysis came back with signs that while at the center she had been using buprenorphine, a drug that can stop cravings when taken regularly.

Buprenorphine is Suboxone, and it is often prescribed to help addicts live normal lives after addiction. But not at the Lapp Center, at least not then. At that time in Vermont, buprenorphine in the form of pills, "bupes," was being sold illegally, and the government warned of its potential for abuse. When someone would crush and snort this drug on her own, when it had not been prescribed by a doctor or dispensed by a pharmacy, that was taken as a sign of continued substance abuse, because in some cases (but not normally) buprenorphine can produce a high. This is not something I understand perfectly, given that I have been told that buprenorphine omits the high but addresses the craving. And so I do not know if Jane was seeking a high or attempting to control her addiction on her own. One doesn't know the intention of the user, whether she is a woman scrambling to stave off cravings until she can get the real drug in her system instead of seriously seeking out treatment, or whether this is the act of a woman betrayed by the system who needs to work out her treatment on her own.

Her testing positive was not the end of Jane's stay at the Lapp Center, however. They would have kept her there, but Jane checked herself out, reporting to her therapist there as well as to her own DCF worker that she was too anxious to be locked up and "monitored constantly." As the Lapp Center is a place for mothers and children together, when Jane left, Tessa was returned to foster care with her older sister and brother and Allie, her foster mother.

I knew these facts, not only from Jane but from the written DCF reports, and they had been conveyed to me, in a high-pitched, agitated voice, by the guardian ad litem, a person assigned by the court to investigate what is in the "best interests of the child" in a custody case. In Jane's case, there were reports of fights with different boyfriends. There was an earlier report by a good psychologist, one who knows not to go beyond the evidence in an evaluation, which stated that the psychological testing gave us nothing to go on because Jane was too "guarded" to give honest information. There was a mysteriously brief letter in the file from Jane's time in therapy in which a drug and alcohol therapist wrote that Jane had had eight sessions over a twelve-month period. At each session her toxscreen was clean; however, she cancelled these sessions so often it took an entire year to get eight sessions with eight accompanying toxscreens in to DCF.

The avoidance is what began to win out in my memory of Jane. Jane is avoidant. She sought out bupes on her own, without talking to a doctor. She cancelled therapy appointments constantly. She gave up at the Lapp Center after five days. She ran from that Ohio hospital. Was this the avoidance of an addict, a person with crippling anxiety, a mother with deep mistrust, or all three?

I have to admit, when I sat across from Jane, I was rooting for her. I liked her more than any other mother I'd seen who was fighting to regain a child she had lost. She was different from the spunky adolescent-like women who'd been through a lot but had kept a sense of humor and an aura of fight. She was a mom, constrained, focused on her daughter. Although Tessa had been in foster care for almost two years, she knew Tessa's quirks and abilities and she delighted in her accomplishments. She admired her two-word sentences. She cared if her visits with Tessa went well for Tessa's sake and wanted Tessa to feel at home in her home. She was focused on Tessa's responses to her and her visits and not on proving to me that she was a good mother. And she won me over when she answered my Solomon-like question: what do you think should happen to Tessa?

The Solomon question. I didn't call it that until I heard Jane's answer. It's from the Bible story of two women fighting over an infant who then turned to King Solomon to decide who would have this baby. The king slyly proposed to split the child in half and give half a child to each mother. The true mother of the child, the one Solomon chose in the end to care for the child, was the one who cried out "no," the one who gave up her petition in order to save the child's life. One has to ask though, why didn't the other mother cry out? Because she was a bit smarter than the other one, and raised an eyebrow to old Solomon, thinking, "What's going on here?" But the point of the story is well-taken in modern motherhood lore. A "true" mother is the one who puts her child's needs ahead of her own—one more way women have been made to feel guilty for wanting careers. There is a conspiracy of blaming mothers for anything that befalls their children. And if we are good enough, we respond with motherguilt. Motherblame and motherguilt go hand in hand, and we are answerable to men or the state or some other authority.

Jane answered my question, "I'm worried about what the guardian ad litem said about attachment. I don't want Tessa to have attachment issues. If coming back to live with me will harm her, I don't think it should happen. I know it's up to you to tell us whether it will harm her. I want her to come home, but not if it will damage her for life."

We looked at each other with tears in our eyes. I didn't sense that this was a woman who knew the right thing to say, or a woman who was ambivalent about the return of her child. Well, maybe a little ambivalent. What I saw was a woman who loved her little girl. I wanted to help her.

So I listened with an open heart to the stories Jane told of therapists (most likely interns) who have come and gone in her life, never really there for her; the stories of losing homes, one after another; how difficult it was to get disability; which lawyers worked hard for her and which ones shouted at her in the courtroom; the DCF workers who judged her from the start and didn't listen. Sitting across from her, I began to get the feeling that a huge injustice had been done to this woman, who most likely had a history of trauma, although she shied away from sharing anything about her childhood with me and nothing about trauma was in her file. Perhaps she was wise not to share that. Jane was certainly a woman who had been traumatized by the loss of her children. No wonder she didn't trust DCF, therapists, or the government. She had been hurt multiple times, and loss may be harder to master than abuse. I wanted to hold her hands or put my arm around her bony shoulders to tell her I would root for her. But something held me back.

At home, with the DCF case plans scattered around me, Jane on paper felt different to me. Less like me, and more foreign. She had an addiction that she didn't admit to. And I no longer trust myself around people with addictions, having been fooled by an addict before—my son.

Because of her addiction, some "facts" about Jane haunted me: Why did she run from the hospital in Ohio while Tessa was still there, recovering from jaundice? Why didn't she want to work with the DCF worker who found her there? Why did she start therapy so late? Why did she miss so many therapy appointments? Why did she end her therapy when Tessa was still not back in her custody? What kind of attachment was she able to form with her therapist? How did she, according to her own story, quit her addiction on her own? Why didn't she have an addiction story, with relapses, support systems, struggles? All addicts have a story of how they quit. Why could Jane quit so easily when my own son had struggled so hard, with relapse after relapse?

I paused on the question about Jane's therapy. Attaching to a therapist is a good sign. It would show something about Jane's own attachment history, how she was mothered, which would say something about her capacity to mother. I also have a strong bias that psychotherapy is good and that everyone should try therapy. When I hear that someone I am evaluating is invested in therapy and has a good relationship with a therapist who wants her to succeed, I feel warmly towards her. I see her as wanting to change, as able to tolerate the tough feelings that arise in therapy and willing to process some of the trauma that got her where she is today. It helps to see her in a meaningful and deep relationship, a consistent one that demands a regular hour every week.

But those DCF files told a story about Jane's therapy that was different from one of a consistent working relationship. In the file it was noted that Jane did everything she could to get out of it, dragging her eight sessions out to last an entire year, and showing up for eight sessions as this was the bargain made with DCF and the therapist, at least eight.

When Jane finished therapy, Tessa was twenty-one-months old, and she was now two years old. Fourteen months in foster care is the time at which the government thinks a permanency decision should be made. Children need permanence. Any fourteen months will do.

From one year to two and a half. From zero to fourteen months. Maybe a disruption wouldn't be as horrible for a fourteen-month-old as it would be for an eighteen-month old, or a twenty-one-month-old, or a two-year-old. Maybe that's why fourteen months is the magic number. But a toddler will suffer from the separation, and Tessa was now two. Should Tessa be moved back to Jane's home for a trial period? Away from her foster mother, the only mother she has known? For the visits she's had with Jane surely must feel merely like playtime with a nice lady.

I stop breathing when I think of such a loss, the way it might be experienced by the child in the weeks and months that follow it, a loss she most likely will not consciously remember. I feel nauseous when I think about the foster mother who will be experienced by Tessa as an abandoning mother, wicked, unloving, a betrayer, though all the while she has been fighting to keep her safe.

But I want to be fair. I am not as sure as the guardian ad litem, who believes that moving Tessa now will cause irreparable damage to the child's attachment system. Considering all the overseas adoptions of children of variable ages, the facts are not with the guardian ad litem, and perhaps thankfully so. Attachment disorders are rare, and they usually are associated with unstable infancies, full of adversity. Children adopted from overseas may develop attachment issues at greater rates than non-adopted children, but the majority of them do not. And I was put off by the hysteria in the guardian ad litem's voice on our phone call, wanting to be fairer to Jane because of what seemed like a system stacked against her. In the end, however, I needed to produce a just assessment in the best interests of the child, no matter my reaction to Jane or the guardian ad litem.

The paradox was that in the two years that had passed, Tessa's foster mother had taken too good care of her, and Tessa, by all accounts, looked to be what is known as a "resilient child," less fragile than other foster children, robust. In a case like this one, a child's strengths become her vulnerabilities. Ironically, both her care and her development went so well that it suggested she would suffer a loss better than most children, and so she could be made to suffer.

But suffer for what and for whom? Who's to say it is in the best interests of a child to be with her birth parent? If Tessa had a say, she would have chosen to stay put where she was, with her foster mother, Allie, and her two siblings. She might have even argued that Allie is the best parent to help her deal with identity issues in adolescence and enable her to get the therapy she might need in the future. Allie is the parent she is calling "Mommy." But judges seem to sometimes decide that the rights of birth parents should take precedence over what a child wants, even though the law strictly speaking says "best interests of the child." I have seen plenty of parents who got a raw deal from the state, but we don't make reparations for this by awarding them their child.

Tessa is only two. I can speak for the child. I can speak about her best interests. But I have to be truthful. I am stuck with knowing that the court doesn't care how much she might suffer as long as there's a good chance she will someday bounce back from the trauma of being sent back to her mother, if her mother is well enough to help her through the transition. It all depends on Jane and whether I trust her to be telling me the truth. I kind of know she isn't. But I don't know how wide the chasm is between Jane in person and Jane on paper, and I probably never will.

As a reader, a scholar, a mother who cannot even tell when my own child is lying, I choose the Jane that's described on paper. This means that Tessa will stay with her foster mother. She will stay with her siblings. Hopefully, she will still see and know Jane as they both grow older apart, and hopefully Jane in person will stay as lovable as she appeared to me in my visit with her, because that too would be in the best interests of the child.

3. A CHILD IN A BOX

"Remember our rule," I tell my husband, Paul. "Nothing goes into the basement anymore. Things only come out." We're not hoarders, but we both agree that certain things may be useful in the future. Old silverware, for example. You can give them to your kids if they need them or set up a summer home or bring the extra forks upstairs for a party. And empty boxes. Come the holidays, we won't have to pay for post office boxes to send presents to our children in Texas and New York; our siblings and nieces in California, Oregon, and Illinois; my best friends in Chicago and Seattle. But now I won't let him put another box in the basement alongside dozens of empty boxes and crates filled with mouse-infested children's clothes, originally saved to one day give to our grandchildren (because their daddy wore this when he was little). We've given up fighting the mice, who seem to be building nests even in my file cabinet of old evaluations. We're empty nesters and they're nesters.

Adele nested in a packing box during her observation visit. Four years old. Hiding in a box from her foster mother, desperate to be found. Merry, her foster mother, noticed but seemed to find this bid for attention a bit of a nuisance and sought a spot where she and I could speak in private.

Adele and her foster father, John, were very close, and I was at their home to determine whether I would break up this budding father-daughter romance and return Adele to her mother, whom DCF thinks may be ready to parent her child. John had become so close to Adele because she adored him, but also because it seemed to balance the family that had become lopsided after the birth of a son and the intense mother-son connection that had developed. When John and Merry's son was six, and the pattern of closeness between mother and son with dad on the outside hadn't changed as Freud had predicted it would, the couple considered adopting a child. Adele was four years old at the time.

Their son, Garrett, was a beautiful, cared-for, easy child, a green-eyed child with sand-colored hair, a child who basked in unconditional love and so was able to love his little sister with ease and no competition. Adele had been in their home for eighteen months, and Garrett joined his parents in praising her accomplishments and helping her master four-year-old tasks.

"Mommy, Mommy, pack me up and send me somewhere," Adele cried as we passed her hiding in the box, the two of us deep in conversation about Adele's adjustment as the observation visit came to a close. Foster children aren't permitted to call their foster parents "Mommy" and "Daddy," but try telling a four-year-old that. This is especially true when other children are in the house.

There was no "There you are!" from her mother who was attending to me and my observation visit. So I stopped, kneeled beside the cardboard box, and asked, "Where do you want to go, Adele?" Was it her wish or fear or possibly both to be packed up for a UPS pickup and, what, sent to another foster home? Returned to her mother? How did she know what this visit was about?

Her foster mother, Merry, had admitted that Adele was hard to figure out. Adele was sometimes "aloof" and sometimes "oppositional," perhaps afraid to yield to the lovely mothering Merry had to offer, holding back to preserve her relationship with her birth mother, whom she saw once a week in prison at a two-hour supervised visit. If she stayed close to her nonthreatening foster father, a man who came alive in the glow of her admiration, she could have both/and—she could be loved in that foster home without needing to let go of that other mother, the visit mother, the one who holds her tight and cries, the mother she barely remembers living with. Adele was two when she and her mother were separated and her mother went to jail. And this was not her first foster home.

I wanted to play with Adele, close her up in the box and pretend to send her away, just for the drama of it. I wanted to see where she thought she was when I opened the box and said, "Here you are!" In play the emotions wrapped up in being sent, given, or abandoned could emerge in a way she could tolerate. It's just play. And yet not just play. If I closed the box up, could she, for just a few seconds, tolerate that alone and trapped feeling that the closed box might elicit in order to arrive at a moment of being discovered, of feeling wanted, when I opened the box and marveled at what was inside. "It's Adele!" But in an observation, I could only watch the scene unfold. Adele frowned as her mother and I passed the box, walking into her foster parents' bedroom to talk alone, out of reach of children's ears.

Is it enough that Adele's foster father and brother adored her? Will Adele attach to Merry once she has more fully lost her own mother, if she does fully lose her? Will she attach out of desperation or relief? Or will she reject this new mother over and over again to exact revenge on the imaginary mother, the mother who robbed a convenience store for drug money and went to prison. I once met a little boy whose birth mother had tried to kill him. In his new, safe adoptive home, with a mother ready to love him and care for him for years to come, he refused to ever meet her eyes. He would not allow a caress at bedtime. He would not speak one word to her. He settled into his new home, speaking with his adoptive father and the brother who had experienced the trauma with him but was responding differently to it. There was not much this new mother could do to earn the boy's trust. She simply needed to remain her gentle self and keep trying.

After meeting with Adele's biological mother and putting her through the hours of testing, I was unsure she could care for Adele, and in the end I recommended that Adele be freed for adoption. This is what DCF was recommending anyway. The foster family, I heard, was overjoyed. But I don't know if I put Adele in a box or if once adopted she would keep herself closed up in a box, waiting to be sent to a new home, hiding from Merry. I don't know what happened. Did Merry find her? Did Adele let her? Most evaluations end with a report that DCF uses to inform their decision. Some end in court, but if they don't, I'm no longer needed. I make recommendations but rarely know the outcome, whether DCF or the court has followed my recommendations. And I rarely know the more important outcome—if I was right in my judgment or tragically wrong. I know that the stakes are high, and I am almost always unsure.

4. EXPERTS

Lawyers always want me to be more absolute than I am willing to be, than they themselves are. They are 100 percent on one side, which supposedly is the way our system works. On a phone call the night before court, a lawyer will summarize her perspective to me: "She's lost a child before; we don't have evidence that she's not taking drugs; she's refusing to go to therapy; the kids are in a beautiful adoptive home and doing well; she's had two years to improve, but she relapsed last summer; she's dating a guy who's known to be a drug dealer—she can't take care of this child." The lawyer is giving me her opinion, but she really wants me to be as clear and concise as she is. She is offering what I can say without telling me to say it, and my back stiffens. Every piece of what she says is true, but I don't want to reduce this woman to those facts, and I don't want to destroy a person, any person, even in the best interests of the child. When I speak in court, the mother will also be there, watching me.

I want to be fair, nuanced. I want the judge to consider the great play session I observed between the child and her mother in my office, the mother's tragic history, her earnestness in wanting to quit using drugs, to see it all as I do, even if I will ultimately urge the judge to terminate parental rights. For in the end, I'm with that lawyer when she says this mother can't take care of the child.

I must admit I don't recall what I swear to in court when I am taking the oath. Is it to tell the whole truth and nothing but the truth, so help me God? Or am I remembering an old rerun of the TV show *Ironside*? I'm pretty sure "God" isn't mentioned in courts in Vermont. Nor do I recall a Bible. I raise my right hand and swear something that is consistent with what I want to do, so that is why I don't need to remember the exact words. I tell the truth. That's who I am. But not always all the truth. Sometimes the lawyers stop me, and I let them. It's their story to create, not mine.

They used to scare me, the lawyers for the parents who would use any means to demean me, question my judgment, and embarrass me on the stand. But they don't anymore because they never ask me the most frightening questions: How did you do as a mother? How are your own children doing? If they do ask something personal, anything at all, I know now to sit patiently awaiting another lawyer's objection. The state's attorney or the lawyer for the children will jump up and cry out, "Your honor, Dr. Lamb's life experience is not relevant to this proceeding. She has already been accepted as an expert witness and is here in that capacity."

I've learned that a lawyer who wants to have a conversation while I'm on the stand is trouble. If an attorney is friendly, even curious, my guard will be up. What are they trying to prove? What do they want to extract?

"Dr. Lamb, your resume is impressive and has an extensive list of publications in the area of girls' development and sexuality. Isn't that correct?" This one wants to prove I'm no expert in attachment.

"Sharon . . . May I call you that? You include giving advice to your clients as part of your evaluation, do you not?" That one wants to prove I do not respect the boundaries of the evaluation.

"Dr. Lamb, on page 2 of your CV, you state that you taught at St. Michael's College. Can you explain to the court what you taught there and its relevance to your expertise?" That one just wanted to delay the trial by going through my CV page by page. The judge told her that he was ready to approve me as an expert and she needed to move on.

I am the expert, the lawyer who has prepped me reminds me again and again. For an hour or two in court, I guess I am. But then, on the long winding Vermont roads back from some courthouse in the Northeast Kingdom or Central Vermont, I drive past the blur of snowbanks and trailer parks, RV lots, and tiny post offices. The poverty reminds of where I came from. The hollow eyes of the mother in the courtroom, still on my mind, bring me to consider not my performance as an expert but my own performance as a mother. And I wonder just how expert I am.

How did I get to be an expert? The judge has made me one, over and over again. But I'm not a professional expert; I'm an academic, a developmental psychologist, a counseling psychologist, a therapist who has worked with children and parents for years. I happen to have had a lot of training in testing during my internship years, training I hated because I wanted to be a humanistic psychologist, one who saw the whole person, and found no joy in pinning diagnoses on people.

There are some psychologists who specialize in "forensic psychology" and are trained with regard to a number of legal issues to speak to in the courtroom. They can give testimony as to whether someone is faking an injury or a delusion and if someone is competent to stand trial. There are specialists whose only work is to testify on cases in which a particular expertise is needed, as with discrimination in the workplace. There are also people like me who could be considered an expert in a number of fields because of years of practice, scholarship, or teaching.

My first expert appearance was as a specialist. I had been trained at Massachusetts General Hospital in Boston to do sexual abuse evaluations and had completed a postdoc at Children's Hospital in the area of family violence. I had published one or two articles at the time on sexual abuse and so was called upon to evaluate a little girl. When I moved to Philadelphia, a lawyer found me. Was I, a new professor at Bryn Mawr College, the best expert on sexual abuse of preschoolers? Not by any means. But I knew enough about both sexual abuse and preschoolers to answer the judge truthfully when he asked, "Doesn't every four-year-old girl say they had sex with their fathers?" "No," I said.

In Vermont, it took me a while to get my bearings, my confidence shaken from the denial of tenure. I had worked so hard for seven years, published a few articles, and had a book coming out with Harvard University Press, but I was denied tenure because of a "question of fit," according to the haughty six-foot and blond Main Line college president. "Fit" meant "class" to me. I was lower class, unacceptable to private-school-educated girls, as well as to the poised, tight-faced administrators.

Getting everyone in the family settled in Vermont around my new job in the psychology department at St. Michael's College was my first priority. But after a couple of years, I sent out a little brochure about my new practice that indicated I had done some forensic work in the Philadelphia area. Attorney Jan Cooper called to describe what was to be my first forensic evaluation: A little boy who had been in foster care too long. Parents with a history of domestic violence. They couldn't live with each other and couldn't live without each other. After working with the Philadelphia lawyers, I found Jan to be a revelation: here in Vermont lawyers could slow their pace, take time at their desks in the courtroom rifling through their files, favor flowered tops and sensible shoes over black suits and heels, while also being able to zero in with the precise and perfect question when the time came for it.

After Jan's case, I was hired, on her recommendation, by a couple of state DCF offices. Vermont lawyers are on some kind of email listserv where they praise and trash us evaluators. After I ended up supporting one father's rights, I started being hired by parents' lawyers too, and this was good. If I only worked for DCF, there could be an assumption of bias.

Lawyers tend to think that all experts are hired guns, that many are biased against fathers, and that most do the bidding of whoever hired them. More than once Jan has remarked in passing that I produce unbiased reports, as if that is a rarity among psychologists. Do other experts really bend the truth? I have studied some of the other experts' reports when asked to review a case, and I don't see it. If I read between the lines, I am able to sometimes see that experts who are hired by the parents' attorneys might not want to recommend that the children be returned to the biological parents, but that they are wary of saying so outright. I can see this in the way they suggest more time for the parents to change, more resources for them, more support, and I know that they know that in asking for more time, they are actually saying "not yet," which will probably mean "not ever" for a child who's been in foster care for two years. They have given the DCF lawyer room to argue that enough time has passed and these children need stability.

All of us are supposed to put the best interests of the children first, even when we see that the parents have been treated unfairly or, on the other side, even when we see how adoring a foster father is and how heartbroken he would be to lose this child. It is not our job to rectify a mistake or bias of the system but to say what is best for these children at this moment in their lives.

"My degree is in human development from Harvard University; my dissertation on children. I teach Life Span Human Development, Counseling with Children and Adolescents, and, once in a while, Personality Assessment. I train students to be psychologists and mental health counselors. I trained at Mass. General Hospital in the Child Psychiatry outpatient unit, with special training in family therapy, sexual abuse evaluations, the Rorschach, and divorce and custody evaluations. I did a postdoc in the area of sexual abuse and family violence at Boston's Children's Hospital. I've seen children in my practice, at least one or two a week, for thirty years. And my dissertation advisor at Harvard was one of the leading critics of attachment theory." There you have it—the short speech I give, when asked, to describe my work, my expertise.

This last point about my dissertation advisor, Jerome Kagan, is important because I have not published directly in the area of attachment. It's not my academic specialty, although I teach and train master's and doctoral students on attachment theory. Some lawyers look at the long list of publications on my CV and ask me to point out which of these are on attachment. Only one entry is on attachment—a review of an edited book on attachment from a global, socio-anthropological perspective, a book critical of the concept of attachment. In return, I can say that my dissertation advisor was one of the leading critics of attachment theory and from him I learned how to understand the problems with measuring attachment. This makes me a somewhat more careful evaluator than some.

My reports are long. I let people tell their stories and summarize afterward: first, the raw data; then, my understanding of it; then, my recommendations. It's a challenge to look through the data I've presented and see if any other conclusion could be reached. If seven family members, in their own words, have said that Mother has lied about Father's domestic abuse and that she left the state with her daughter to be with her new boyfriend who had children in that other state, then by the seventh subheading, "Interview with Auntie Jane," a judge will get the picture before she or he reads my conclusion.

A judge has never questioned my expertise. But I question it all the time. There are always those more expert or at least more confident in their expertise than I am in mine. I do have the research skills to wade through good and bad research on a topic and discover what science has to offer. I have yet to find research that shows as decisively as the court would like me to be that a child will be harmed by an attachment disruption, or by a parent with an addiction. I can only speak to risk.

Maybe my feminism makes me an expert on mothers, although that is one criterion neither the lawyer nor I will bring up. It would certainly be seen as a bias rather than an asset. I see how much we expect of mothers and how little we expect of fathers; the greater stigma there is for women who are recovering alcoholics and addicts. I am also suspicious of a system that sees trauma as only debilitating and not something that can make a woman stronger. I do not underestimate, however, the cumulative effect of sexual harassment, abuse, assaults, and all the other traumas the mothers I interview have endured, traumas that can lead to the "poor choices" they are personally held responsible for. I am in the confusing place of wanting to support women while at the same time, quite possibly, making a recommendation that will hurt them more than any trauma that was inflicted on them. In my expert opinion. In my humble opinion. As a mother. As a mother who has lost and then found her own child—that particular trauma. I give an expert recommendation.

5. BOUNDARIES

At night my thoughts are too filled with the people I am evaluating. In the weeks during which I am performing the evaluation, I think about them in my sleep and wake up thinking some more. It's not like solving a crossword puzzle, where I can consider a clue, leave the *New York Times Magazine* on the kitchen table, and go about my day, letting the clue drift in and out of consciousness until the right answer pops in. It's more like being filled with the life of someone else.

I was trained to be empathic, as I train my students to be. One might ask whether it is possible to train someone to be empathic or whether it is a quality one is born with. As with most nature/nurture questions, the answer is both/and. Empathy has several components. First, a person must be alerted to someone else, pay attention to that other being. In the day-care centers where I did research in my early years as a professor, when a child fell and began to cry, some children, but not all, would look up and over, alert to the sound, and just gaze at the other child. Others would not only gaze but would orient their bodies towards the other child. This was remarkable given that crying in a day-care center is a common occurrence. They oriented towards the crying child, but did they care? Once or twice one would approach the crying toddler and offer a blanket or a toy.

My younger son, Julian, needed more of a boost to be empathic, distractible as he was and more readily irritated by someone else's cries of pain. So, when he was little, I would over-emphasize my pain when I bumped my head or tripped and fell, in order to draw attention to it, and then I would praise him mightily when he showed concern. I think it worked, but maybe I didn't exactly teach him to be empathic, only to understand his natural agitation at another's pain and to help him reshape that reaction as empathy. His natural irritation was a good thing, because it showed an alertness to the emotion in someone else that could be shaped. Research suggests that after alerted to someone else's pain, the next step requires that you put yourself in the place of the person with a general accuracy about what the other person is experiencing. It does no good to feel sympathy for a person in pain if the person turns out to be doubled over in laughter.

In my internship class, I practice doing this with my Mental Health Counseling students. They are often afraid to make a mistake and so resist my suggestion to do a role-play, which is when one student plays the client and the other student the counselor. No matter how much I remind them that they are beginners and still learning, and reassure them that they shouldn't expect to be perfect, they still feel frightened and ashamed if they do not "say the right thing" when playing the role of the therapist. In a sense, they are right to be frightened. Being able to express empathy is not only at the core of therapeutic practice but, really, of life for those who think they have been called to this profession. If my students think that they are found wanting, they will likely feel as if they are not adequate as people, not just as therapists, not good enough.

Sometimes I playact the part of a client and ask the students together to throw out one-line reflections of the client's emotions, the goal being accuracy. I create a narrative based on a client I have seen and wait for a response.

"You were feeling frustrated," says one student.

Frustration is not a great emotion to zero in on. "Go deeper," I say. "Frustration can sound like a minimization of anger or disappointment."

"You seem to have thought that that person was criticizing you."

Better. But I tell this student that he is analyzing a thought rather than reflecting a feeling.

"You were hurt," a third student says. Bingo.

I tell my students that the very basis of psychotherapy—forming a working alliance and gaining the client's trust—is accurate empathy. It's incredible when a simple empathic statement about how a client must have felt in a situation hits home. The clients of therapists will encourage their therapists along, particularly young ones, whether their therapists are accurate or not, saying, "Yes, that's it," so I tell my students not to depend totally on the client to tell them when what they've said is accurate. Clients will often make do with what they get while they work at getting their stories out. But when a therapist says simply, "I understand. You must have felt so . . . ," there can be a connection like no other, a communing, and a relief.

After accuracy, empathy requires that you care. Researchers may disagree with me, but accurate perspective-taking, without empathy, is cold, whereas empathy is warm.

Too much empathy, some will say, is a problem. I don't agree. I think that the problem isn't too much empathy but inadequate boundaries. When one person is stirred up by the life and emotions of another person, sometimes it is difficult to separate oneself from the other. The therapist might shed a tear at what her client is talking about, but if she is crying harder than the client, feeling the pain more acutely, something is wrong.

Psychoanalysts call this "countertransference"; however, the term "countertransference" has also been taken up by therapists of all denominations. It can mean a number of things, but its most simple usage refers to when a therapist feels emotions based on his or her own life or personal history, or when a therapist responds to a client based on the therapist's needs rather than the client's. A therapist can have a "me too" feeling, for example, or can be overly invested in what a client should or shouldn't do, and that's quite normal and natural. Therapists are taught to analyze these reactions so that they can see them clearly as they arise and not act on them. Acting on these feelings, not feeling them, is the real problem, resulting in a boundary crossing, sometimes a boundary violation.

The detachment needed to be a good therapist and still an empathic therapist is difficult to achieve. In my work as an evaluator, I must always be vigilant to not punish a mother as I might punish myself or rescue a child who reminds me of my son; to not overvalue a father's contribution because I miss my own father, to not undervalue a child's love for her mother because I don't recall the loving moments between my own mother and me. I am not always successful at all of these, but I check myself, before writing, before going to court, and, hopefully, not after.

6. THE CHILD WITH A TINY BLUE PIANO

I do cross the occasional boundary. That particular day, I wasn't in the home on behalf of the scrawny four-year-old foster child who wandered the house with the small blue electronic piano keyboard in hand. His eyes were huge, his clothes too big for him. I was there to talk to the foster mother, Joan, about a different child. Like many foster homes, this one was a menagerie, with blue-tongued lizards in heated glass cages, several cats and dogs roaming, gerbils and hamsters on their wheels, a goat in the yard, and finches multiplying as we spoke. Foster parents seem to need to take care of things, as many foster homes have a great number of animals. I'm okay with the cat hair and the dogs who boldly snoop back when I snoop in their homes, their noses in my computer bag, my crotch. Petting them gives me comfort.

At this visit, the four-year-old walked past me and his foster mother several times, ignoring me, as if he knew I was there not for him but for his younger foster brother. He carried the little blue keyboard with him as he strolled the pattern of the walkway between hassocks, chairs, tables, and couches. The "piano" he was carrying had tiny buttons that a child could press to hear individual melodies, and this child kept pressing the same button over and over. It was Mozart, and I tried to remember the melody so that I could check back with my husband when I got home to ask him to name the piece. He can name that tune in four notes for most classical music. It was a teensy tinny movement with lots of runs. I had heard it before, but it wasn't a standard like "Eine Kleine Nachtmusik" or some other common tune co-opted for use in an advertisement or a toy.

He listened and walked to the beat, playing it over and over. And when he put the piano down and picked up a sad-looking coloring book with stereotyped girls picking flowers and stereotyped boys flying kites, I heard him sing some of the melody, on pitch, note for note in the mellifluous run exactly where all the notes should be. I asked the foster mother about him.

"I don't know how long he'll be here. He loves music," said Joan as she shooed the German shepherd mix away from my computer. "He seems to have some musical talent. He's really good with that tune," I said, wanting to let her know that he should know, too, that he is good at that. Somebody should know that. When he walked by, I hummed a little of the melody at him, and he looked at me and hummed it back.

I have a vivid memory of my son Willy at six. Paul was playing a Brahms theme and variations, and Willy stomped down the stairs that were situated behind the piano singing the melody loudly to the syllables "Da, da dum, da da da dum, da da da dum," then "Du dah, da dum, da da da dum, da da da dum." It was a complicated, almost atonal melody that had authority. For me, it closed an invisible lasso around the two of them, musical ear to musical ear.

Sometimes I want to give kids more than my evaluation. I imagine taking the money I receive from an evaluation and giving it back to the parents or foster parents and saying, "Use this to start a college fund," or, "Buy a used car with this" (yes, I make enough on an evaluation sometimes to pay for a used car). I want to bring hand-me-downs from my own boys to give to their little ones or go out and buy some cute Baby Gap outfits to dress them in. I want to bring the huge bucket of Legos I keep, even though my children are grown, and give it to a little builder who doesn't have more than a Zip-Loc bag of colored bricks that he carries with him from home to home. When a child loves a toy in my office, I want to say, "Go ahead and take it home."

I can't do that, though. The rules of professionalism prohibit these kinds of boundary crossings. Not as strongly as they do boundary violations, but they prohibit them nonetheless. They are seen as inevitable but also potentially confusing to a client. And it says something about you in general as a therapist, your lack of trust that therapy is enough, and your longing to be something more to your client, if only for a moment. These boundary crossings can be noted and discussed with a client as part of the therapeutic relationship. In an evaluation, however, you do not have that ongoing contact in which the boundaries are tested and reconfirmed and even talked about.

This time I crossed a boundary, against my better judgment. Agitated with the thought that the other little boy, the one with the blue piano, had a talent that wouldn't be nurtured, convinced that he should have the same lessons and CDs and band instruments and concerts that my children had, I decided I could do something behind the scenes. I called his DCF worker and told her I wanted to pay for piano lessons. I had found a teacher in that town, someone my pianist husband thought was skilled enough as a teacher of young students, and I told her that I would send her the check if DCF could arrange for this boy to get a lesson once a week. The DCF worker was on board with this arrangement and discovered that the foster mother, Joan, was willing to help by taking the little one down the road a bit, where there was a church with an old piano in it, to practice. The only hitch was that the boy might not be living in her house for very much longer. He might be returning home.

I was crossing a boundary I'd never crossed before. Why now? Why for this child? Why was music so important? My own house is strewn with instruments, like the animals in Joan's house. We have several guitars, a euphonium, a slide trombone and a valve trombone, a trumpet, three pianos, probably a kazoo or two, recorders, maracas, and, once, a ukulele, a beautiful rosewood one I bought in Hawaii. We have amps too, small practice amps, guitar amps, and bass amps. I used to say that learning to read music was as important as learning to read. Having acted out scenes from *The Sound of Music* with friends in the fourth grade, memorizing all the words to Maria's songs, I hoped I would have a band or a small chorus at home someday when I became a mother. Marrying a pianist was a big start to that dream.

I bought some of those instruments twice. The second time was after they had been pawned at our local music store. The rosewood ukulele had been snapped up quickly and I never saw it again. I do want that ukulele back. And if I can't get it back, I want to buy my child another ukulele and hear him play "Somewhere Over the Rainbow." So instead I buy another mother's boy piano lessons and place my bets on him.

7. FATHERS

I have to watch myself around the dads. That's another area where I need better boundaries because I sure do like the bad boys, and that's what these dads often are—their energy, their sarcasm, the aggressive life they bring into a room. I like the game some play to manipulate me, and maybe I like the power I have over them. I also, sometimes, want to help them and be their mother, scolding them or sympathizing.

My students don't understand how I can sit in a room with a sex offender or wife beater and enjoy his company. It's not that I believe their denials or their minimization of the violence they perpetrated, except on occasion. But they are more than that. And for some of them, especially the old Vermonters, I enjoy listening to their big tales: "I've broken every bone in my body"; "I was a captain in the marines"; "I was the one who told the senator to . . ."

My own dad was a big talker and a know-it-all, the dad whom I loved and looked up to as a little girl but whom I loved and mocked as an adult. He was the kind of man people called a "character." I forgave him his ridiculous pronouncements about the best way to make scrambled eggs or the truth he wanted to tell me about what psychologists do: "They just say 'uh huh' and nod. I can do that. Watch." The joke was that even if that was all that psychologists do, he couldn't sit and listen for more than thirty seconds. And when I went to Harvard he would often say with a nervous laugh, "And by the way, don't forget your old man is smarter than you."

I'm a part of my culture, too, the culture that doesn't blame dads for not being there, for not supporting the mothers of their kids, for not sending child support. As with most women, the strongest aphrodisiac I know is a man taking good care of a toddler. I see this with my students as well, their crushes and adoration of the good men in my department at UMass Boston—the professors who are gentle, who listen, who care about their past traumas, and who are the fathers they never had. We women professors have it rougher, always at risk of being found to be the not good enough mother.

I have supported some fathers but not others. I think that what divides the supported from the rejected is whether or not they have been there, consistently there, in their child's life. Do they show up for their visits? Did they take care of their children when they were small? Do they know their kids' interests? Have they stuck around? Have they tried not to be a disappointment? Have they succeeded in not being a disappointment?

The stout man with a disability who makes a bit of cash sweeping the town's grocery store and has only just learned to manage his own money—I supported him because he fought, for years, to have visits with his daughter, and he took advantage of every opportunity that was offered to see her. Monitored in a church basement, once a month during one year, then once a year during later years, he was on the phone with law enforcement when the child's mother took her out of state. Whatever time he could have with his daughter, he would take.

I also supported the man who banged up his father-in-law's Cadillac in a rage with a baseball bat. He wasn't a great husband and definitely was not a great son-in-law, but he seemed to be a great father, if it is possible to separate all of these out. So it was hard to understand why the judge denied him visits with his daughter. He was in recovery and trying not to drink. Why prevent him having visits with his little girl as long as he wasn't drinking and as long as he stayed away from his father-in-law? And if he did drink? If he relapsed? I may sound lax, but if we removed children from all the homes of people struggling with alcoholism, it would be hard to find enough foster homes for these kids. It is difficult to be the child of an alcoholic. But until someone has given me an indication that the parent has been too drunk to care properly for the child or was drinking during a visit, I can't see removing all access to a child and limiting their time together to an hour a week in a church basement.

I supported the father whose wife was so fearful of his anger that she would only transfer her daughter, Tina, for the "Vermont summer with Daddy" at a police station midway between Plainfield and Albany, New York. I interviewed the little girl, and she enjoyed her summers with her dad. This she told me carefully, secretly. But most of all she looked forward to seeing the same friends she played with each July and August, her Vermont friends with names like Sunflower and Verbena. I understood her mother's fears, and I tried in my report to be reassuring, to say that the Joe she knows is not the same Joe that is father to her daughter. The Joe she knows, who is furious that he is monitored by the police and will snap at the new husband who's replaced him, is not the Joe who makes large Bread and Puppet Theatre–informed papier-mâché animals with his daughter or who plays duets on the recorder with her.

What fathers have I not supported? The ones who disappear and reappear, in and out of the child's life, who say that they thought the child was doing well with the new stepfather and so didn't need him, the one who seemed like a nice guy and who I never would have imagined would slam his son's head against a wall when angry. The ones who say they didn't realize their girlfriend was depressed, their baby wasting to nothing: "She just cleaned the apartment a lot." The ones who started a new life, with three new babies, with someone else and then swooped in to claim the son he never visited, just when DCF was about to free this son to be adopted by the foster family who now treasures him. The ones who don't show up and then do.

I don't care so much if the dads yell (my dad yelled all the time), or if they swear at the kids (Paul occasionally swore at the kids, his sophisticated mother from Vienna swore at hers), or if they spank them (my mother spanked me, but I was duly cowed by just the threat of a spanking). Fathers who are angry are commonplace in our culture. I read about all the angry fathers in my students' papers on attachment, what made them the way they are today, what family dynamics, what kinds of parents. The angry father is a trope and a reality. While I understand and sympathize with the wife who finds the anger abusive and terrifying, I'm often not quite sure at what point the anger becomes abuse to them, and whether the anger became abusive to them because it has triggered other memories. I just don't trust the phrase, "He was abusive," without further evidence.

I ask myself, Was Paul an angry father? As I do not let myself off the hook, how could I excuse my partner, my collaborator? He was angry, a grumbling dad, like in movies where the father is the only hold-out against getting a dog. He was also a loving father. And in the end, we got dogs. When I ask if most fathers are angry, am I justifying patriarchy? Excusing it? I was right to leave Willy's biological father, a boyfriend at the time, and he was right to leave me. But why did I marry Paul, who at first had no strong desire to be a parent but was happy to come along for the ride, admiring Willy from afar as Paul's father admired him.

Paul is Willy's father. There is no doubt. By a shared love of Jewish comedians. By hearing the same phrasing in music. By adoption decree. By a hundred bath times. By a thousand drives to extracurriculars. By a million worries. From fifteen months old, Paul has been in Willy's life. Willy knows no other father. He has put in the time, showed up, stayed. The two of them are father and son, but to me, Paul was always a choice I made to give Willy a father, and a choice I would reconsider in bad times. He was also whom I chose to cling to in the middle of the night when we both were awake with damp dread.

8. A FATHER FROM THE PAST

Sweaty and hot, the man leaned his bike against an overflowing recycling can outside my favorite Starbucks and gulped water from a plastic biker's bottle. "Hi," I said, rather warmly, thinking, I know him. He stood there, frozen, staring at me. Then I remembered how I knew him.

"This is a challenge for me," he said, wiping his shaved head with a handkerchief. "I'm standing here thinking that this is a challenge." Yes, *that* father. This was exactly how he spoke to me once in my office when I interviewed him. He was so open, sharing his emotional experience, then in an instant he would distance himself to analyze what he had just said, closely monitoring our interchange, trying to read me.

I stopped smiling. This happens to me every so often, running into someone whom I've evaluated but not realizing in the moment how I knew him or her and trusting my instinctive feeling about them, like a happy puppy jumping up to greet everyone. It is true that a Vermonter is constantly running into people she knows. No longer able to trust my memory for names, I tend to just smile and follow my inclination, warm or cold, waiting for the other person to tell me how I know him.

Sometimes, though, I know the person through Al-Anon, and she'll stare back at me meaningfully, not really wanting to say out loud in front of my friends, her friends, or anyone else around how we know each other—"anonymity is the key to all our activities." And sometimes it's through my therapy practice and I saw the person in a session a while back but have forgotten her.

"I'm sorry," I said, trying to indicate that I knew now what I didn't know a moment ago. "I hope you're doing all right," I added, knowing that I also hurt him with my evaluation.

"I haven't seen my little boy."

I knew that might be the case.

"Is it okay for me to tell you something about your report?"

It was 89 degrees, and my dog Iko was in the car waiting. His snout was sticking out of the window sniffing Starbucks smells and more. It was also three weeks after Lara Sobel, the DCF social worker who had been involved in a case that terminated a mother's parental rights, was murdered by her client, shot outside the DCF office. I hesitated, but I wanted to hear what he had to say. I've always had this idea that if I welcome someone's anger and truly listen to it, that he will be soothed.

I should have known better. At one of my husband's concerts, a college newspaper photographer was taking photos while he was playing the first movement of a Hindemith sonata. As usual, I couldn't listen very well because I was concerned that Paul was distracted and getting more and more crazed by the clicking sounds of the photographer who was roaming all over the stage during the performance, crouching behind the bassoonist, looking over Paul's shoulder at the score. On stage at the end of the piano, the photographer lowered himself slightly in order to take a photo of Paul through the space between the strings and the lid. The audience was distracted by him, but Paul and the bassoonist continued. When the movement ended, Paul paused and stared at him. The audience was completely quiet because the musicians had stopped and gave no indication they would go on. I moved up to the stage and motioned the student over. I told him I was the pianist's wife and that he should wait until the musicians were bowing at the end of the piece before taking any additional photos. He came down from the stage, stomping a bit as he sputtered self-righteously, "I have a right to take photos. I work for the *Guardian* [the school newspaper]." I saw how agitated he was—like a child—and put a hand on his shoulder and said, "It's okay," to which he yelped, "Don't touch me." He then proceeded to walk up and down the aisle saying, "She touched me," and, "Do not touch me," and, "She had no right to touch me." As he was off the stage, the musicians began their second movement, but he was unable to stop what soon became a rant about touching and the rights of journalists. I stepped out into the lobby hoping he might follow, though he didn't, and called campus police, who kindly waited in the back of the auditorium until the piece ended before approaching the photographer and walking him out of the hall. I later heard that the young man was unable to finish the semester.

The lesson I learned, I suppose, is not to touch people without asking first. I also learned that not every agitated person is soothed by a maternal approach or even perceives a maternal approach as maternal. I continue to believe that kind feelings and warmth can be healing outside the therapy room as well as within. But why even persist in that belief? They surely weren't enough to help my own kids. And they confused the father standing in front of me at the Starbucks.

"Is it okay for me to tell you something critical about your report?" he asked politely.

"Yes, of course," I said, glancing at my car, registering Iko's black nose.

"You said I was a narcissist. Nobody, anywhere, nobody who knows me, nobody thinks that's true." He then listed several important people in Vermont who did not think he was a narcissist. "So you see, that's a mistake in your report, and it's just wrong. I hope you don't mind my saying that to you. Is that inappropriate for me to be telling you this?"

I didn't recall writing in the evaluation that he was narcissistic, and I didn't recall thinking that he was a narcissist. I wondered if a pencil and paper measure, like the MMPI-2, suggested this as a possible diagnosis, and if I'd felt compelled to type this diagnosis into one section of the report as a possibility. I kind of remembered the day in court and vaguely recalled that the lawyer went to town on something or other that made me squirm, maybe it was "narcissism." Lawyers love diagnoses, thinking that they are some proof of mental illness, which is then proof of inability to parent. That is so rarely the case. Maybe the lawyer was trying to prove that because one test suggested narcissistic personality disorder as a possible diagnosis, this man was unfit to parent. But that was not my thinking at the time at all.

I said, "I'm so sorry about that. I don't remember. I don't like diagnoses, so are you sure I said that? I'm really sorry." I didn't remember that. But I remembered *him* now.

He asked, "Can you redo the testing? I never got to say everything I wanted to say." He had lost his son, but not because of his psychological make-up or the results of the testing. There were far more complex circumstances that could have led to him getting a raw deal. Still, he wanted me to correct the report, as if it existed as some lasting mark against him, like that imaginary high school "permanent file" that perhaps still contains the information that I once forged a note from my mother.

Or maybe he just wanted to correct what he thought was my impression of him. I recalled that I had spent more time with this father than any of the fathers I have evaluated, so his feeling that he didn't get to say everything he wanted to say was telling. His life's story, I now clearly recalled, took him across the world, to Africa, through Asia, for a time in Belize and through several fascinating relationships in each before returning to the country roads of Vermont.

"You can hire someone else as an expert," I offered. "That happens all the time. That person can do their own testing and refute what I said in my report."

"But you can't do it?" he begged. Oh, I had made a connection with him. It wasn't the public record he wanted changed, a record that was closed anyway because it involved a minor. He wanted me to change my mind, wanted me to see him differently, not that I even saw him as a narcissist. The warmth I felt towards him at our initial greeting was now ambivalently reflected in his request to see me again.

"No, not me. It can't be me. I'm sorry. My dog is in a hot car right now and I have to get to him. But try to remember all the good things I said about you in the report. Please try, and try not to over-focus on that one aspect."

As I backed away, he asked, "Was it inappropriate for me to ask that of you?"

"No, no. Of course not." I wanted to add, "Let it go," but I know from experience that those three words mean nothing to someone who can't let something go. And don't I know it. I wanted to tell him to talk about this with his therapist, who may now think that I view this man as a "narcissist" and that I am a poor psychologist, but how can I control what anyone says about me to their therapist?

"All right, thanks," he said, looking relieved to have me remove this challenge from in front of him.

I haven't used that word again, "narcissist," although during the beginning of the Donald Trump presidency, psychiatrists and psychologists were slinging that word around while at the same time condemning each other for using it. Who can judge another's egocentricity? Even the Rorschach people no longer find this dimension reliable. Who can separate narcissism from self-preoccupation, vulnerability, shame, performance, braggadocio, denial, or well-deserved pride? Who can separate the person from the projection?

9. THE RORSCHACH

A bat. Two overfilled couches, their stuffing coming out. Crocodile heads, snapping. And there, right there, a British man with a top hat, on a bicycle. A face of a sad woman. A child crouching with a guitar. And maybe just black smoke, like "Smokey" in the TV show *Lost*, moving in like fog.

Trying out a game called Blotto or Klecksographie, as it was called in Switzerland, the psychiatrist Hermann Rorschach first noticed that his patients with schizophrenia responded differently to the blots in the game than did other patients. Later, working in a Russian hospital with adolescents, playing once again the game of Klecksographie, Rorschach created forty blots and regularly used fifteen of them with his patients. Over time he collected responses from both patients and non-patients, and he focused not on what they saw in a blot but on what characteristics of the blot they responded to. For example, did they use the color in some of the blots to lead the way to a perception? And did they focus on the tiny, tiny specks coming off the main appendages of the central form or take in the whole and try to make sense of it? A publisher agreed to produce a set of ten but added shading to the solid colors upon printing. Hermann liked this, and the first set of inkblots was published in 1921.

Several systems used to understand the responses of people viewing the Rorschach inkblots were developed to address the criticism that psychologists were reading into what people were saying and producing horoscope-like interpretations. The Comprehensive System brought together several systems in 1973 and was the most popular coding system until recent improvements on it by the Rorschach Performance Assessment System team.

There has been considerable controversy about using the inkblots in court. The psychologist presents the ten designs to a person being evaluated and writes down what the person says he or she sees in the blot. I don't think most people describe everything they see. I wouldn't. And one of the secrets of the test is that it doesn't always matter so much what you see. There are other things we are looking for. Top-secret things. Things that if I told you might lead to my expulsion from the Rorschach email listserv, where psychologists dedicated to the Rorschach share their tips on scoring and justifying the Rorschach in court. I took a vow of secrecy when I ordered my pack of cards. But that hasn't prevented their appearance on eBay by less responsible and rule-bound psychologists nor a pretty concise summary of them on the internet.

Somehow just an image of the blot has come to represent "shrinks," a term that usually refers to psychiatrists who typically don't get training in Rorschach administration anyway. It's we psychologists who get that training, depending on the doctoral program. And because there have been valid criticisms that led to the Rorschach being questioned in court, a new cadre of psychologists has done the research and developed a new system to correct its flaws.

The Rorschach allows me to understand a number of things. I can grasp more completely the pain and distress a mother may be experiencing and the way she might cope with this pain. Is it overwhelming her? Or is she shutting down and tuning out? If she is clamming up in response to the hurt, I understand that to be a primitive way of dealing with stress, one that will backfire on her and which leads me to expect her not to be tuned in to the emotions of her children when they get overwhelmed.

The Rorschachs of many mothers I've seen show intense longing and few inner resources. I use that phrase, "inner resources," a lot. Can she cope with stress? Can she cope with life? Does she have stuff within her that she can draw on? Some smarts? Planning? Patience? Creativity? Good, solid internal parental voices giving advice? The ability to reach out? Logic? Emotional vitality? The ability to use emotion in her thinking? The ability to use reason with emotion? Stuff. Good stuff. Great stuff. Where can I buy some of that stuff?

When you are in crisis does all that good stuff go out the window? Like the time my husband and I were puttering around in a motorboat too close to shore and we hit a rock. When the motor died, my husband yelled out, "Now we'll never get back." We were twenty yards from land.

Why did my husband panic? His first response is often not his last. My first response is to take charge and issue orders. This surely happens with many couples. Paul is emotional. He often gets overwhelmed with emotions, touchingly when listening to the romantic aria in Verdi's *Un Ballo In Maschera* (A Masked Ball), movingly when discussing the effects of what climate change might mean in the lived lives of people in the future, and annoyingly when I am trying to fall asleep and he is talking about our children. This is, however, an essential quality to being a musician, and music organizes his emotions in some way I don't understand but is good. I have thought about my therapy clients and their relationship to art as soother, as provider of order, as nurturer. It is there and true for many.

I haven't given the Rorschach to my sons. Willy would score high on the Rorschach item that shows a person tends to live in a fantasy world, that he'd rather dream a solution than enact one. Julian would perhaps show too much emotion and reactivity to emotion, a tendency to react to it in spontaneous and uncontrollable ways. One son holds emotion in. The other lets it out. They are both incredibly intelligent: Willy self-undermining, Julian more self-expanding. I pushed the older one to act in the world. I made the schedule and drove him up and down tedious Vermont roads, demanding participation in jazz band, lessons, camps. But he has increasingly retreated into a small protected space. I tried to temper the emotions of the younger one and teach him to manage them, but he is big and irrepressible in both difficult and marvelous ways. This quality has brought him deep, generous friendships, most of which he formed at Grateful Dead–related concerts and festivals, supported by experience-enhancing drugs, I am quite sure.

My Rorschach, I know, would show a number of internal resources, a file cabinet full of them, an ocean of them, a universe. I would be an actor, not a dreamer, but someone whose anger and emotions and whose impulsivity and reactivity can interfere with good personal relationships. Self-esteem would be low or maybe just high enough. And there would be a ton of people in the Rorschach cards that I would see: people dancing, playing, working together, singing, but also arguing, fighting, competing, in a tug-o'-war. Look over there, at the side of the blot, in the green and pink, there's a mother dragging a child to do something he doesn't want to do!

One mother I tested showed nothing and yet everything. She could barely give me enough responses to result in a valid protocol. A bat. A bat. A moth. A bat. This one's hard. I don't know. Colors. A bird. Paint on the page. She turned each card over and set it down quickly, as if looking at the chaos of the ink was just too much for one person. This is a typical response of a woman who is afraid to let me in or who has either very little within or is afraid to look at what's within.

Another mother had to be stopped when she gave me so many responses. "Look at this one. I'm flying over grassy fields. Look at the flowers below! They're beautiful. Poppies, like in *The Wizard of Oz*. Those are exactly the poppies from *The Wizard of Oz*. They are more poppy-like than the poppies in *The Wizard of Oz*." She slams the card down and onto the next: "Oh my, oh my, I get a dark, terrible feeling from this one. Something bad is about to happen here. It is just ominous, ominous. Do you know that kind of feeling? Can I move on? And here there are two children together singing at the top of their lungs, dressed in costumes from the nineteenth century. I think they're in a play together. These are colorful streamers hanging down for the performance, and below are some frogs playing the saxophone to accompany them! It's a party. A wonderful frog and human party."

This mother is responsive and reactive and most likely takes her children on some wild and imaginative rides through life. She responds to color, as well as to the black of different blots. But where are her boundaries? When depressive feelings surface in response to a blackish blot, she can't even organize it into a monster or a black cave. It is just "a dark, terrible feeling," but the feeling is powerful and has movement. And when she sees color again, she integrates the children with the play and the costumes and streamers but doesn't seem to care that frogs don't really play the saxophone nor join humans at parties.

None of these in and of themselves are worrisome responses. All the responses taken as a whole and the repetition of oddities are what make a Rorschacher alert. The mother who could integrate so much in such a powerful way might have done fine had her children not been suffering or had powerful needs for stability, soothing, and structure. She had inner resources to offer them of one kind. The strict, religious, and slightly depressed father of their children had resources of another kind. Both should be able to serve their children well as parents, together, if not in the same household.

The Rorschach is filled with twists and turns. For one mother I write, "While Danielle may have an adequate ability to reflect on herself and others, this is compromised by a distorted and limited view of others." She has the capacity to think about others, their motives, their insides—but she probably gets it wrong. I write, "While Danielle can show flexibility in thinking, she may be under-responsive to the vitality that life has to offer." Such a thin line—to be open to the vitality that life has to offer and not to be overwhelmed by it, the color, the shading, the movement, the love. What are you picking up on? What are you responsive to? Can a song move you? A pink and coral sunset? And if not, why wouldn't you be responsive? Because your mother hurt you? Your father kept you in a cage? Because you spend too much energy protecting yourself, surveying the environment for signs of danger?

I don't think I am as open to the vitality that life has to offer as I should be. How many of us are? I know that I spend too much energy protecting myself, surveying the environment for signs of danger in the form of other parents. The danger, of course, is in my own projections of their perfect lives, their perfect parenting. Sometimes too much to bear.

10. OTHER PARENTS

I have never seen uglier furniture, I think, as I enter the Al-Anon parents' meeting, projecting my state of mind onto this new blot. I am not here to observe a client. I am here for myself, and I am vigilant. A black rocking chair with fake gold paint along the edges. A couple of puffy sagging chairs in big flowered print from someone's home. A bunch of green cafeteria chairs. There are people in my response to this projective test and I perceive them to be worn out as well, in a Vermont, end-of-winter way, wearing drab sensible clothes this Sunday. I note one cheery woman whom I have seen here before and who talks too much. I regret when she enters the room or rather, in Al-Anon lingo, "these rooms," as in "these sacred rooms." I resent her, although I am aware that others welcome her. So it is my problem. But she suffers so little these days from whoever's drinking or addiction that her addict rarely features in her stories. In Al-Anon that shouldn't matter as "we keep the focus on ourselves and not our qualifiers because . . . ," something about accepting the things we cannot change and knowing the things we can.

There are a couple of other people who have maintained their looks through their crisis. One mother who always comes looking smart and tidy with her husband. I like her because in spite of her put-together appearance, the hurt and anger at her daughter that she voices feels raw and real and is the B-side of her husband's hurt and optimism. I am drawn to the down and out, to the most resentful of us petitioners.

I don't enter "these rooms" as a therapist but as a supplicant. In a very real sense, these are now "my people," even the ones I don't care for, as I avoid friends whose children are leading professional and interesting lives, friends whose conversations always veer into a socially accepted version of bragging or whose simple remarks like "I used to play on the floor with my children all the time" I perceive as bragging. Not just bragging, but as some condemnation of me and proof of yet another thing that makes me a not good enough mother.

I have found something in these rooms. It isn't God, that projection of evenly hovering attention. In Vermont Al-Anon it is fine to call one's higher power Goddess, Great Being, or even Great Pattern. It's okay to think of it as a voice of clarity within you or even to see the Al-Anon group itself as your higher power. See what you want to see or imagine what you want to see. Take away from each meeting whatever works for you. This seems to work well enough for most of the nonreligious people I have come to know at this meeting, because in Al-Anon, we need to admit that we are helpless and turn over our control to something outside ourselves. I try.

I am late to the meeting and seat myself outside the circle, behind a woman with a nice haircut, dressed in the trendy, fine clothes people buy up in Montreal rather than down in Vermont, a cashmere scarf tossed on the floor next to her chair. I think, this woman looks particularly natty, and when she speaks, I discover that I know her.

It's Sofia, a former friend I had dropped because the success of her son had been too much for me to bear. And here she is, at an Al-Anon parents' meeting. How sad for her, her husband whom I also know, her son. Wow. I guess none of us are spared.

These are my people now. Not my former friends and especially not the parade of good enough parents who come to our house bringing their children for piano lessons with my husband, Paul. He only accepts children who show talent, discipline, or a sparkling interest in music; for me, it's a set-up for a troubling comparison. The parents want to chat and show polite interest in our children, enter into the easy conversation in which many parents engage, sharing children's accomplishments and parental worries with the warm expectation that I will share back and that there will be an exchange of admiration. There is an expectation that all loved children in musical households turn out fine.

These parents feel in control of their children's lives, feel responsible for them and their outcomes, as I do or have done. Pride and shame are two sides of the same coin. I do not go to book group for this reason, after an evening in which the accomplishments of the children of the women were just too hard to hear. One son won a Pulitzer Prize, we were reminded again. Another has a son with a PhD from Berkeley. A third, a child who's an editor in New York at a major publisher. Their second sons and daughters are accomplished as well: teachers, activists, journalists.

I know that each is one cancer diagnosis, one car accident away from joining the likes of me and my husband, but for the time being I have formed other friends, women whose children are in trouble, one with a DUI, another with two children he can't support, another mother with a child who may be charged with attempted murder after a bar fight, and another mother whose son had a psychotic episode while roaming Europe, not answering his parents' calls and emails. We get together to not talk about our children, but do anyway.

I wonder if I am a little pleased that Sofia is here. I guess I am. I am pleased that among the dirty furniture and the Sunday sweatpants, the clogs and Crocs of Vermont folk, I have a new compatriot, a friend in the wasteland of people who have to choose their clothes every morning, who have to choose to even care. Another mother. And when I consider her situation and find her good enough, perhaps some of that generosity will return to me.

11. A MOTHER AND HER SON

When I arrived at the first-floor apartment, part of a white clapboard leaning house, #3 Warren, there was no doorbell to ring. I tried the screen-door handle and it was locked, which I guessed meant that someone was inside. I walked alongside the house and saw that the shades were drawn and the windows were closed, so I rapped on one and called in, "Hello, are you there? It's Sharon." Someone yelled, "Just a minute" and then a woman opened the front door. It was dark inside, and James, the boy I was coming to observe with his mother, was watching a video while also playing with six Matchbox cars. He jumped up when he saw me and asked me to come play cars with him. I said maybe at the end of my visit but that first I needed to type on my computer while he played with his mother. That was actually a big hint to James's mother, Rachel, that she might play with him, a hint I don't usually give before a home observation. But Rachel sat down away from James and leaned on the armrest of the couch. She told me she had just woken from a nap.

It was one of the only gorgeous days of the summer of 2013, a summer that featured rainstorm after rainstorm. The land was so soggy it wasn't until August that Frenchy, the man who brush-hogs our fields, could mow down the weeds. I regretted having to be inside on such a wonderful day in such a dark apartment and asked Rachel if she had been to the farmers' market, which was only two blocks away. She looked at me as if she had never heard of it or of farmers' markets generally, and so I told her about what the market was like, what they sold there, and how it was a short walk from her house. She had been out to Hannaford's instead that day, a huge grocery store, a drive away. On the counter between the room in which we sat and the tiny kitchen, there were the spoils of her trip: peanut butter, Mountain Dew, Cheetos, coffee creamer, and cigarettes.

I didn't really care and wasn't planning to tell on her. Some weeks my diet is the diet of my childhood, with pop and Fritos and even cupcakes edging out the proteins and vegetables I'll force down. Some weeks I am good and go to a farmers' market and make interesting food centered on whatever is local and fresh, ready to look up what to do with a pound of black radishes.

I liked this mother, kind of. Almost as much as I liked James, her son, who was five and bright and agreeable. At my office the week before, her IQ tested at 71, and that made me protective of her, less judging. She seemed depressed though. And I had a hunch she had been quite neglectful of her children, which might be why her other children were not living with her. I knew that her mother had recently died. She told me that she thinks about her every day. I remembered that phase of life, after losing a parent, and how each parent, even the one I had rarely thought about, my mother, began to slip into my life again.

I made myself comfortable on a folding chair next to her couch. She asked about the tests I had given her: "How'd I do?" I was worried about how I was going to explain about her IQ. Two points lower and she would be eligible for so many services. But two points lower and she would have to make sense of an identity most individuals would be reluctant to embrace.

The apartment was small, about the size of many a trailer I had been in—bedroom, bedroom, living room, half a kitchen. But it was clean and painted nicely. James returned to his car play with the TV on showing a video of animals busy solving puzzles, eager to learn in a make-believe town. Rachel's feet were up on the hassock and James moved towards her and sat between the hassock and the couch, leaning on her legs like a drunk at a bar at the end of the night, running the little cars up and down one of her legs, then standing to follow the trek of one blue Camaro across her belly and over her chest. Clutching a car in each hand, he used her two legs as roads. Beep beep. Occasionally she reached down and gave him a tickle, and I marked that down in the notes I was taking on my computer. Affection! But mostly she watched the video in front of her.

James tired of tracing roads to nowhere on his mother and brought me a hand-held mini-computer that had games on it. These are "laptops" so small that a preschooler can hold them. This one had an alphabet game. The player was to watch a letter of the alphabet progress across the screen from left to right and then find the letter on the tiny keyboard and press it before the dancing letter reached the other side. O. Q. R. B. He showed me how it was done, and I almost couldn't resist a word of praise but I held back. It was an observation, so I gave the game back to James, and he put it down on the couch and went back to using his mother's legs as highways for his cars. Sometimes if I praise a child, the child will start orienting all his play towards me instead of interacting with his mother, and this was a situation in which I thought that might be possible.

Rachel picked up the game from the couch and began to choose the right letters. She delighted in the game. For the last half hour of her one-hour observation with her son, she played the alphabet game, letting James know each time she passed a level: "Mommy passed a level!" and saying, "Good job!" to herself.

The observation finished. I wanted to cross a boundary and take them for a walk, buy them a homemade chocolate chip cookie from a stand at the farmers' market nearby where two darling girls in aprons and braids took their business quite seriously. But I took a walk in the lovely little town on my own. I bought a latte, that symbol of frivolous need of the upper-middle class. I found some buttercrunch lettuce at a stand and bought that too.

I drove home passing a horse barn so long I decided to count the windows across: twelve. Like James's mother, I found some pleasure in simple counting. Simple games of recognition. Learning. Repeating. Knowing. At any level.

That night Paul and I were going to our friends Molly and Ari's house. We were bringing champagne and homemade ice cream. I was looking forward to playing a little bit with her boys, Noah and Quinn, before they went to bed, because Molly and I often talk about our children, and I have known them since they were babies. I recalled when Noah was five years old, the same age as James. Sophisticated and smart, Noah could not only recite the names of planets but tell you their order and whether they had moons and when the latest ones were added to the solar system by astronomers. I think he had a telescope. If not then, he certainly would have one by now. He had books on the solar system that he brought over to show me. He had seen Venus! With both parents professors, his access to a wealth of knowledge was incredible. James, at the same age, seemed already so far behind. There is no meritocracy, I think, even though I was once a child of a depressed mother, playing house with crayons of different colors representing mother, father, sister, brother, because we had so few toys.

What might happen to James were he to stay with his mother in her small apartment with the windows closed to the world outside? Will he get enough stimulation at school? Will his teachers see his spark of curiosity? Might they love his agreeableness, his affectionate nature, his fine attention span? Thank God for schooling. I loved school. But I was a girl who could take that love through high school, college, graduate school. How many years will teachers have with James, to nurture him before he draws the shades, shuts the door, and locks them out as boys can do? Will those years be enough if there is so little to stimulate his mind at home? One Christmas he will receive an Xbox and *Call of Duty* or some future representation of these hypermasculine toys and all that quickness, awareness, eagerness will have a focus. At a later Christmas, he will tell his mom he is joining the Guard, not that he is going to college. And as a father he will be eager and aware in the woods, hunting with his own children. He might not have the opportunities of other children, but if he is lucky, that spark of interest I saw will be kept alive.

I probably offered my children too many things I wanted them to love because I loved them. There is a bedroom full of books that I hoped they would read, but they mostly didn't. As a child, I loved being around books, even though no one else in my family was a reader. My favorite day of the week was when the Bookmobile came to Dodge Avenue and I got to choose as many as five books for the week.

I wasn't just sharing my love of books though. I gave my sons everything I thought that I could have had and would have had as a child had I been born to other parents, educated parents, parents who read, who knew about the world, who knew facts. Parents like Paul's parents. Marrying Paul, I learned about how upper-middle-class Jewish New York childhoods went. While the books I smuggled under my covers were Scholastic Books, three for a dollar, and my parents scolded me for reading too late, Paul's parents gave their children the classics to read, in hard cover, with inscriptions on the inside cover. I begged for piano lessons when I was fifteen and got them. But Paul's parents gave piano lessons to all their children, as well as swimming lessons, skating lessons, horseback-riding lessons. Back in Chicago, my friends the Fink twins were astonished when in seventh grade I confessed to them on a field trip to the Art Institute that this was the first time I had ever been to an art museum. Paul's parents' apartment looked like an art museum; his aunt was an artist, with a studio and her own paintings in museums.

But the more lessons, camps, books, and education I bought for my sons, the more they turned out to be regular kids who wanted to play *Need for Speed* on the computer or *Grand Theft Auto* on PlayStation. They didn't seem to have the longing I had had for all these brilliant things: art, music, literature, learning. How do other parents accomplish this? I see they do, but I don't know how. Private school? Fancy camps? I didn't want to raise snobs and I didn't. They're smart, regular, funny guys who learned as much from *Seinfeld* and *Curb Your Enthusiasm* as they did from watching me or Paul.

Maybe James can learn from the TV he watches too. Maybe his little screen with the silly alphabet game on his handheld system will satisfy for now, given his mother's enthusiasm for it. Will he continue to be hungry for that sort of thing, or will his interest in learning fade over time? The nonprofit Campaign for a Commercial Free Childhood asks that parents cut down screen time for children and provide them with toys that invite children to use their imagination. But

I wonder if this is predominantly a middle-class parent's concern. Good enough parents will keep the screen time to a minimum and create in the corner of their playrooms or child's bedroom a spot with a magnificent dollhouse and an elevated train set. And good enough parents' children will build block towers, make up stories, play dress ups, listen to music, press stamps with ink, and place puzzle pieces. But if screens are there, children will watch them. As one who was brought up with the TV always on, I know how comforting the buzz of the TV is. To me it signifies Daddy. It suggests the open space of the night, when my mother was in bed and my father watched old movies and reruns of *MASH*, when he did the *Tribune* crossword puzzle and snacked till he fell asleep on the couch around four or five in the morning. In spite of the TV in my own childhood, I learned vocabulary. I learned to read. I developed a sense of humor, quite possibly from Buddy and Sally on *The Dick Van Dyke Show*.

My report will say that James should stay there with his mother, that his mother should have more resources to match her abilities, that his mother should have therapy for her depression, her grief, and that James should have all the extracurriculars that other children have. It will say quite simply that James is attached. Maybe James will learn a thing or two on his own. Maybe he'll pick up on a few new words in Busytown or master saying "please" and "thank you" as the animals do. Maybe he will act in kind ways towards others as the animals do, or solve a friendship problem, as long as it doesn't ask for more effort than is shown in the little drama of Busytown. I certainly wanted more for James than that, but I couldn't give that to him. I could recommend he stay with his mother and hope that the safety of her solid figure on the couch in front of the TV would be something sustaining to return to as he began to confront the world beyond those window shades. I could hope.

12. MOTHER AND CHILD AT THE BEACH

"We're going to the beach!" Ridley yelled out when she saw me. Thin and jittery, she approached, then retreated, then approached again, meeting my eyes. She was yards away from her mother, who stood constrained with a fierce smile carved into a flat face. This mother had been clean for six months and wanted her daughter back. Standing next to Ridley was their DCF social worker, who seemed to approve of this plan.

A walk to a beach for an observation visit isn't too unusual. Outings give me a chance to evaluate a mother's ability to plan ahead. And planning ahead is one of those things mothers are supposed to do. Before visits, the mothers' social workers advise them to be sure to provide food and other necessities their child might need during visit time. I can then evaluate how well this coaching has worked. Does a mother remember the diapers and wipes for an infant? For a toddler, a bottle and a hat to shield his lovely tender head from the sun? For an older child, water, snacks, and a few toys? No mother remembers everything, but given the importance of the visit, the performance of being a competent mother who remembers everything is what's required.

When I require mothers to have one of their visits at my office, for a second observation, after having observed them at their usual place, they typically arrive with big backpacks and floppy, overflowing shopping bags. Children who are used to the visit routine hug their mothers quickly and then dive into the bags as if it were Christmas morning. Will there be a present or a favorite snack? I have seen a child collapse on my office floor in disappointment when a snack she had asked for wasn't there. I recall another child obsessing for the entire visit about the promised snack that did not arrive.

"How many times have I told you to bring the *white* cheddar cheese Cheez-Its? You never listen!"

"But they didn't have any at the gas station on the corner."

"You should have gone shopping on the way!" one child wailed and hit his mother on the chest. Having had to plan for himself in the past when under her care, he may have become a better planner than she ever was, whether or not he had the ability to carry out the tasks.

"Ridley, this woman is here to watch us *be* together!"

Ridley was already in the house, looking in the refrigerator to see what was there. "Cheese sticks! Good. You did good, Mom."

They packed the cheese sticks in the cooler and the four of us left. As we walked to the beach, Ridley and her mother skipped ahead swinging the cooler between them. Mom had packed towels, water, and suntan lotion. Nice planning, I thought. I, on the other hand, had none of those but, preserving a boundary, I didn't want to ask to borrow anything, even later on the walk when I felt my nose starting to burn.

When the lake was in sight, Mom ran into the water splashing sparkles of water up around her like a silver aura. As the water got deeper, she switched to swimming, moving far away from all of us to the deep end of the swimming area marked by a three-sided dock. We watched her swim beyond earshot until she reached a dock and, holding onto its edge, waved to the three of us on land. Ridley stood at the shoreline in her baggy bathing suit, like a lonely figure watching a boat disappearing on the horizon. She dipped one toe in and withdrew it. Then she entered the water, step by step, letting the chill come and then diminish on each vertical inch of her body, until she was neck deep.

How could I do my observation, sitting on the beach, so far away? It was a challenge to interpret what might have been their particular mother-daughter dance: Ridley taking her time, Mom enticingly waiting with sparkles and joy in the deep end. Was I wrong to expect what I would have preferred to see? More encouragement for the hesitant little girl who did seem, without encouragement, to know exactly the way she wanted to approach the water and was doing so?

Mothers must perform for me. They must perform the roles of "encouraging mother," "helpful mother," "patient mother," "authoritative mother." What kind of mother, during her performance of motherhood, would swim away from her daughter and enjoy herself all alone in the deep, her feet now up in the air as she attempted a handstand. A fun mother? Her long braids were dripping wet down each side of her bathing suit. She had come to the beach to play.

We all perform motherhood in front of other mothers. As my own mother would adopt a certain attitude of restraint around other mothers, I, too, learned to look as if I were under control when I was insecure, giving other mothers my child-psychologist tips on infant sleeping or making insightful remarks about the uniqueness of another mother's child. Underneath, I confess, there was envy, judgment, admiration, but also sympathy, all of it.

Ridley was finally in the deep, holding onto the dock. I rolled up my linen pants to above my knees and waded in so that I might hear the two of them talk, leaving my notepad and pen on the towel. It would look strange for me to stand in the water, in front of all the mothers and children there that day, taking notes. I tried to be discreet but had to yell, "Can you come in a little closer to shore?" They were in a huddle, bobbing in the water, heads together as if plotting their escape. I waited and shouted again. Mother swam over to me to let me know that it was better for me to observe them from afar without hearing them. She explained that it would be to my advantage to obtain a different perspective than most observations, a better perspective by just watching and not hearing. Then she abruptly turned, raised one arm high, and brought it down in a superior crawl she beautifully executed back to Ridley.

I chatted with the social worker on the sand while keeping an eye on the pantomime. When Mom and Ridley finally came back on the beach, Mom spread out their picnic lunch. I hadn't brought anything for myself. I watched them eat their cheese sticks and ham sandwiches and then take turns burying each other in the sand. Mother's inclination to keep her child from me, far off in the water or buried in the sand, was a good one.

What do they matter anyway, these little moments about food, about encouragement, about listening when a child is upset? What do they matter to the whole of motherhood? No mother has the right food for the child all the time—God, the lunchbox items my kids tossed away. No mother always praises her child—I recall a time Willy showed me a drawing and I stared at it blankly, my mind elsewhere, until he said, "Don't you like it?" No mother listens to her child whenever he speaks—"Mom, Mom, *Mom*"—I can conjure that plaintive impatient cry that occurred whenever I was on the phone. These observations mean nothing on their own.

I put down my paper and pen, closed my eyes, and rested my head on my handbag that was substituting for the towel I didn't have. Fuck being prepared. What mother could ever be prepared enough for what her children bring her?

"Sharon, come find me! Come find me!" I opened my eyes and looked over and saw Ridley's head emerging from a sand tomb. "Cara, come take a picture of me on your phone!" Ridley wanted to include us in the circle. When Cara, the social worker supervising the visit, had taken a few photos, Ridley asked her to send them to her foster mother, Diane. Another mother to include.

I remembered what it was like as a child to be buried in the sand, of that first panicky moment of not being able to budge, not knowing if I would ever get out, and then finding that moving a finger made a small crack in the cocoon. I remembered burying my own children and their directing me, "More here," "Get my toe over there." How trusting and intimate an act. What did it mean that Ridley brought to the experience three other caregivers: me, her social worker, and her foster mother. Did this make her feel more secure? Was it a way of reassuring herself that she would be seen, even when her mother tries to take her away to the deep end or capture her in the sand. Does she want to know, after all the years in foster care, if she goes back to live with her mother that the rest of us will still be here? Is she saying, if so, will I be safe?

At home, when the lunch not eaten at the beach was laid on the table with some extras, Ridley cried out in disgust, "I had that last time! You're a terrible mother." Her mother stared blankly. It was clear she didn't know how to respond to such strong and unexpected disappointment, her daughter proclaiming her worst fear, that she was a terrible mother. She knew how to play with Ridley, but it didn't seem to be part of her repertoire to enforce a silly rule that so many mothers enforce: "Eat your lunch. That's what we're having" or "Those words are unkind. Apologize and then eat your lunch."

What might I have done? I probably would have looked through the cabinets to find something different to make. I would have taken the kinder rather than the stricter route. I might have rolled my eyes and mocked my child saying, "Yes, I'm such a terrible, terrible mother because I served the same lunch twice!" But a performance of motherhood means setting limits, and Ridley's mother stood still, not knowing what to do.

There is sometimes a moment when a mother wants to look at me or her social worker and just ask us, "What should I do? What is the right thing to do? You must know. I don't know what I'm expected to do." This can come in a moment when a mother would normally have yelled at a child or removed the plate and said, "Go ahead and starve then!" But a smart mother knows that during a performance, those responses won't do.

Ridley rescued her mother from the deep end and took a bite. And about halfway through the sandwich, she got up and went to her mother and kissed her on the cheek. She then began singing a little Disney song to herself, from the movie *Frozen*: "Let it go."

13. FAILURE OF EMPATHY

I didn't think I liked this mother and continued to wonder as I listened and sipped my water, why not this one? She wasn't so different from the others. She had a horrible history, too, one of the worst, a history that could pull at the hardest heart's heartstrings. Both her parents were alcoholic, physically and emotionally abusive, and her father sexually abused her. She lived in fear her entire childhood, and in high school made excuses to stay at her friends' houses as much as she could. She described her mother as cruel, selfish, demanding, and "unsympathetic." That she said "unsympathetic" chills me most. Her father? "Always angry. Always mean. Always scary." I almost reflected back to her that her childhood was a "horror show," but at the last minute switched it up to "horrible childhood." The word "tragedy" hovered for a moment, but no tragedy yet—it's not over 'til it's over, as they say.

We sat across from each other with our big bellies, the kind of bellies many mothers who live in poverty have when they're not emaciated from drug abuse, the kind of bellies academics develop from sitting at their computers, when they're not emaciated from dieting and fitness regimens. The two of us. Too much sitting. Too much eating junk food. She smiled, and I heard sweetness in her voice that maybe explained the sweetness of her children, the ones the DCF worker said she absolutely adores.

But it *is* over. The state is taking this mother's children away from her and freeing them for adoption. The interview is a final effort on the part of her lawyer to try to get her some visitation rights post-adoption, wherever they land, in the hope that I will say it will be good for them to continue to see her. I'm not sure they can give a parent this right to a visit post-adoption unless it is formalized in a PACA, a post-adoption contact agreement. But if a judge advises it, and DCF encourages continued contact, it will most likely happen. All parties seem to agree that this brother and sister are attached to their mother and that she has something to offer them. This seems easy.

It could have been something about her manner that put me off. She smiled and was polite and told her story as if she were writing my report for me, calling her first husband, "my first husband," never switching to just calling him Mike, so that I had to repeatedly ask her when she said "my first husband," "You mean Mike?" She described her high school boyfriend as a "registered sex offender" who had already been to jail for "lewd and lascivious conduct," a man twenty years older than she was at the time, whom her parents permitted to live in their house in her bedroom with her. When relating about how Mike hit their daughter "about fifty times with a belt" and when he threw her son through a sheetrock wall, she showed little emotion but said, "I couldn't stand it." She explained that every time she would leave him, the kids would beg her to take him back and blame what he did on her. As if reading a fairy tale she went on, "I stayed and stayed and stayed" (and the winters grew colder, the nights longer), and "it got worse and worse and worse." Only when he picked up a steak knife, grabbed her arm tight, and threatened to cut out her heart with it, did something happen. A man was staying with them at the time. He was a friend of a friend who needed a place to stay—there are always so many people sleeping on couches. This man was there at the time of the threat with the knife and gently said to this woman's first husband, not knowing that he would become her next husband, "Hey man, your children are watching." According to her, the abuse slowed after that very concise man-to-man encounter.

I could lie and say that what made me feel differently about this mother, unsympathetic, was the story she told me about her daughter, Lizzy. But that would be untruthful. The story she told about her was one in which she had left the child with her own parents, Lizzy's grandparents, over many weeks. As all parents, rich or poor, know, grandparents are handy for babysitting. But her father had sexually abused her as a child. She stated she was well aware this might be a problem, so before she let her daughter, Lizzy, stay with her grandparents, she prepared her, in case Grandpa approached her. She taught Lizzy what was a "good touch" and what was a "bad touch." She said to me, "I asked her every time she went to my parents' if she knew the difference between a good touch and a bad touch, and she said yes." In her mind, she was doing what she could to prevent sexual abuse.

It wasn't until they were in their own home when Lizzy's brother said at bedtime one night, "Mommy, Grandpa touched Lizzy," that she understood that the same sexual abuse she had experienced growing up was happening consistently to her daughter. Still, she didn't blame herself for such a ridiculously unprotective approach. She wanted me to understand that it was Lizzy's fault. After all, she had done what she could and Lizzy had been carefully educated. Lizzy could have spoken up for herself. But Lizzy was seven years old.

That story was enough to bring down the condemnation of 99 percent of "good enough mothers," but I don't think that that was what was turning me from her. I am used to people reliving their histories over and over, visiting them on their children. In fact, I have heard stories like that before. But the lack of empathy I felt seemed to be more connected to the blank screen of her face: Not coldness. And really not a lack of emotion. But some kind of clinical distance from her life, as if it were only a story and didn't affect real lives, her daughter's, her son's. I knew from my years working with trauma that numbness is a symptom of PTSD and that one of the few ways of coping with torture that is unescapable is to steel oneself against it, even becoming a perpetrator oneself, or to float away and look down from the ceiling at your body being beaten or raped. But that knowledge didn't help me.

It was her language, the odd way she used words as if she had recorded them at an earlier date and was bringing them to mind now. Remembering the day the social worker came to remove her children from her home, she told me that he had said, "Unfortunately, we'll have to take custody of Clay and Lizzy." Clay was Lizzy's brother. "Unfortunately" indeed. And it annoyed me that she described how the social worker gave her a "large pile of papers" that stated how her father had "touched Lizzy sexually." The papers were as irrelevant as the "unfortunately." As irrelevant as the next part of her story about "her current husband," whom I had known for the last seventy-five minutes as Dick.

I am unfair. How could she help but be who she was, given her childhood trauma and the continued torture she lived under with her "first husband" and then her "current husband"? The poverty of white rural families in Vermont most likely affected a series of choices that never really were choices. Involved with DCF from the get-go, her very being had been infused by the social workers' language; she identified with them, the only positive adults to look up to. Maybe it was the only way she felt she could gain control over her own story, by assuming the voice of authority over it. She was a woman whose eyes came alive only twice in the interview: Once when she told me about how in school she "made the honor roll" for one quarter. Again when she recited her disabilities: PTSD, depression, high blood pressure, migraines, and tennis elbow. Or did she light up after I let out a sympathetic "wow" or gave some "tell" to indicate that I was impressed she had made honor roll or with her litany of pain.

It is too easy to say that for the rest of the session she was numb or even that I was numb or maybe that we were numb together. The two of us sat in the fog of a life story that was too terrible to withstand. Perhaps what happened in that session was that she was responding to me, mirroring me as she had with so many social workers—my clinical documentation style, the bland way I ask the questions I should be horrified to ask, the professional demeanor hiding emotion, the way I use the right words for the wrong acts. Maybe she was watching me, the way an abused child watches and conforms to the person who might hit her—the person who might hit her without a thought about who she is and how she might be feeling. That could, of course, be what was happening, but tamped down and numb by the trauma playing out with my son, I didn't realize it at the time.

We experts don't speak very often about our countertransference, the feelings we feel in relation to the stories we hear. Or when we do, we do so among ourselves in protected supervision spaces. Countertransference is rarely recognizable when it is happening. And then it is suddenly made clear. Insight. Many of us in the helping professions have experienced some kind of trauma. We live inside a contradiction that trauma both stays, in the body and the mind, and goes; it is treatable. We therapists and evaluators believe we have moved on from our own traumas and can move about someone else's untouched by it in some magical outer circle that surrounds people and their experiences. But we can't always do that. We sometimes relive our own traumas in those rooms, with mothers and with their children. As we are touched or moved together, we sometimes experience numbness together. No matter class or race or profession, we are poised together, like two hikers suddenly aware of the precipice ahead, looking over the edge into the traumatic memory and thinking we must not fall.

14. TRAUMA

If it is true that traumatic memory is contagious, that parents parent their children as they were parented, that therapists, because they know trauma, have special empathy that heals, then our traumas are connected.

Three Traumas

First, a mother's trauma. Angela's trauma.

Angela rubbed her hands up and down her bare arms but no spark ignited in this mother's large green eyes. She was the kind of mother who forgot, when speaking, that I was there to evaluate her, circling down deep into the well of her childhood to send up bats and spiders in my direction. She told me both her mother and father were alcoholics, "pretty unimaginable" but one malevolent and one benevolent, although I doubted the benevolence and thought that the benevolent one had to be conjured as benevolent when the other one was so terrifying. Angela and her sister were locked in their bedrooms for "very long times." When they were bad, she said, they were made to hold a burning potato, just out of the oven, in their hands. When her mother was really drunk, she got out the spatula and would chase Angela to smack her with it on her back and front, for no reason except that she didn't like when Angela would beg her to let her go live with her father. "Daddy's Little Girl," Angela heard with each smack. If her mother got drunk enough, she would kick Angela and her sister out of the house, and they would go to the garage, making their way into it through a cracked door in the back, wedged permanently open by the junk bulging out, then crouching down in the back with old lawnmowers, bicycles, and garbage bins full of things not worth saving. They would sleep on any square of floor that was smooth and cool and untreacherous, unlike the floors of her home, particularly the kitchen floor, which hid small shards from when her mother threw glasses in anger and disgust. During these rampages, her mother would cry out to her daughters, "You stupid assholes! Fuckers! Idiots. Get out of my house! You don't deserve to live! You're worthless excuses of human beings. Get out of here, you stupid fucking bitches!" Angela recalled that when sometimes she bravely called her mother a "bitch" under her breath, she would then run and hide her little eight-year-old body under her bed and rest there for hours, imagining herself elsewhere, at her dad's, or at the home she fantasized belonged to her schoolteacher, with winding marble dual staircases and vases of roses and, yes, two full refrigerators.

Angela had returned to her mother at the age of six after living with relatives in the Northeast Kingdom, an uncle and a four-hundred-pound aunt who slept on the sofa and so could not climb the stairs when Angela's uncle carried Angela upstairs and raped her with his finger. Back with her mother, and under the rule of the spatula, she was molested again at age nine by a man who was staying at their house, sleeping on their couch. Those couch visitors again. There were often men she didn't know sleeping on one of the couches. Her mother was asleep on the other couch and Angela was watching TV when he reached for her crotch and unzipped her pants.

When Angela was ten, her mother got really drunk one night and kicked her two girls out of the house and said she was going to go live with her sister in New Hampshire. Angela's mother packed up her daughters' things in a huge black garbage bag, mingling the two girls' items together, and left the bag on the front porch. Shuffling her girls out of the house, she locked the door behind them, got into her car, and drove away. They watched her leave with mixed feelings before walking to a neighbor's house and asking to use the phone.

Second, a son's trauma. Angela's son's trauma.

"DCF thinks he was abusive," says Nate, talking about how the Department of Children and Families' social worker thinks about what he lived through with his stepfather.

"What's abusive? What do they mean?" I ask, an innocent again.

"Oh, you know, smashed my head against a bedpost, made me stay in the corner for hours until my legs were shikkling, put me in the basement all night and said I was stupid, said I was stupid about a hundred times, a thousand times." Nate's voice is quiet and distant, the cuffs of his long-sleeved T-shirt grimy with a little blown snot and brown dirt marks. "Save the whales" was ironed onto the front. It is clear that the word "stupid" hurt more than the rest, even the head smashing.

"And you?"

"Me?"

"What did you think? Did *you* think it was abusive? Back then. Or do you think it is abusive now like DCF does?" I match his quiet affect, the pace, the distance. But I ask this last question to see if he himself names what happened to him as abuse, having noted that he first assigned that word to his social worker.

"I don't know. I don't ever want to see him again, but sometimes I'm sad when I think about never ever seeing him again."

"Because a part of you loved him?" I am good with part language. A part of me thinks I am helping. A part of me thinks I am never good enough.

"I don't know." Eyes off to the window.

"What did your mom do when this happened? When your father did those things?" I ask, carefully not using the term "abuse" because the two of us together have yet to establish that what happened to him was indeed abuse. I want to know about Angela. Did she help? Was she good enough?

"She just locked herself in her bedroom with my little sister," he says, his voice bitter. Mothers who don't protect are always worse than fathers who abuse. To children and to the rest of us.

I then ask Nate about the times in which he seems to go off into space. His teachers have said he sometimes is unresponsive in the classroom.

Nate is eager to tell me about this. "Sometimes my mind goes blank, like when I hear, um, *his* name, my mind goes berserk, at first. Then my mind goes eh-eh-eh-eh-eh." He makes a noise like a buzzer and then abruptly turns the buzzer off. The name that sets him off is his stepfather's.

"Eh-eh-eh-eh-eh?" I try to sound like a machine asking a question.

"Eh-eh-eh-eh-eh. It means that something's going to go wrong or he's going to attack. Even when he's not here."

"Eh-eh-eh-eh-eh."

"Eh-eh-eh-eh-eh."

"And then what happens?"

"I don't know, but at school when it happened, and I looked down at my hand, it had bit marks on it. I had bit it until it was bleeding. Do you want to see it?"

I look at his hand and the bite marks on it. "I see."

Third, my trauma. An evaluator's kind of trauma.

I pick up the toys in my office and vacuum the sand off the carpet. I can't support returning Nate to Angela. I will recommend that Nate be adopted, by someone who can recognize and address each post-traumatic reaction, by someone who can bring him back to life when the buzzer goes "eh-eh-eh-eh-eh." I dress the Barbies and put them away in the plastic box. I don't like to leave the Barbies naked in their box, so I pull on their tights that don't fit. Their poufy skating costumes. I pick up the leaves from the floor under the ficus tree. I drive home, on country roads, turning left, then right, past the gardening shop, then right at the big red barn, past the trailer park, then left, past the dog kennel, and then two rights. Up the dirt and gravel driveway, swerving this way, then that way, to avoid puddles in ruts and holes, I'm home in ten minutes. I go to the pantry, so full of everything a child could want, and I take handfuls of popcorn to fill me up. Later I upgrade to tortilla chips. Nobody is home yet to talk to, argue with, pester about putting away the almond milk left on the counter. I sit on the couch in front of the TV watching the blank screen. Then I search for *Law and Order*, which is on some channel at all times of the day. You just have to look for it. *Criminal Intent. SVU*, my favorite. I think it's everyone's favorite. It's very soothing for some unknown reason or because of Mariska Hargitay.

As a feminist, I should abhor the parade of beautiful young women raped and slaughtered in imaginative ways, children too, but I am drawn to the police, the compassionate, smart, and parental officers who protect and seek justice, even though they only show up after the fact.

Am I also there after the fact? Leaving children with their buzzers, their self-inflicted wounds, their ways of tuning out and turning off? They're the ones who continue to suffer, who had to be alert for abuse, had to hide or to leave, at least to leave mentally if they couldn't physically. After the fact. Sometimes I think these parents have ruined their children for life, that there is no getting out of this for the child, only more garages to retreat to, beds to hide under, and empty air to stare into. There is no restarting. No matter who the next parent is, foster or adoptive, nor how much love she or he has to give, the child is ruined. What a terrible word, a terrible thought—*ruined*. Was Angela ruined by her own parents? To be fair, I apply this word sometimes to myself, my own family, my own life. Sometimes I think that I will die before I see that my son is okay, really okay, that my own life and my family's lives have been ruined by drugs and by what I didn't or couldn't do. When I think like that, I run, hide, space out, or watch *Law and Order*. But I have a counter-thought that is as soothing as the end of many an episode of *Law and Order*. This thought is that we are all, right now, in this moment, okay. And I add to this comforting thought, every person, every family has some trauma to live through at some point or other in their history, whether it's a death, a mental illness, an accident. And that second thought brings me back to the present, the room, the TV, the chips, the warmth of a dog sitting next to me on the couch, his head in my lap, the light from the window, the piano being played in the far room, the now of my life. So I grab my phone and text Willy, "Whassup?"

15. KNOWING

I always reached the truth in the middle of the night. That truth was that Willy had an addiction. Depending on whether you believe that once an addict always an addict, he is an addict still. But when he was using, and when I didn't know what I should have known, I always reached any truth about this in my sleep. Only in the deep hours of the night would I know quite suddenly something I didn't want to know. Even then the awareness would come in small chunks, as if my unconscious were feeding me bites of a meal that was good for me but that I resisted, as if a parent were saying, "Here comes the airplane," and as the fork approached my mouth, I smacked my lips tight and turned my head.

Denial started early. There in Mexico, on vacation, Willy, a sophomore in high school then, slipped away in the evening when local vendors were at the resort. I bought silver and turquoise earrings from the vendor and tried to speak Spanish. I asked the vendor if he had children, and he told me their ages. And then he pointed to Willy across the courtyard and asked if he was my *hijo*. I said *sí*, so he then told me that Willy had bought a small *pipa* from him earlier in the evening and might be smoking marijuana. Parent to parent, I thanked him. I confronted Willy later, and he denied it all. So I went to sleep that night not knowing what to believe. Two conflicting realities, one so obviously the truth, and yet I was confused. That night, under the crisp sheets spread tight from bedside to bedside, under the covers that had earlier supported a towel twisted into the shape of a swan, I lay still with doubt waiting for the truth to come. That time the truth arrived back home in frozen Vermont, when I unpacked our clothes, throwing sandy bathing suits and shorts from the children's suitcases down the laundry chute, out came something small and red—a souvenir, the *pipa*.

After that time, I didn't need concrete evidence, a *pipa*. Just patience and sleep. In the middle of the night, again I woke and knew something I hadn't realized in the light of day, that the instruments that had disappeared from our home had been stolen and sold to the local music store. After rehab, Willy told me what he'd done with the instruments. When I went to the store to reclaim them, I was angry with the owner for accepting these instruments. He was offended at my accusation that he took advantage of a kid with a problem. The store takes in many instruments every week, he told me, and they don't keep track of who sells and who buys them. He told me that someone close to him had struggled with addiction, and he knew how heartbreaking that could be.

Still later, the GPS that was stolen from my car, from my CRV that was in my mechanic's driveway, was not stolen. It was stolen. It wasn't stolen. It wasn't stolen by anyone, no random thief. At three in the morning I woke up with sudden clearness that Willy, then in college, had stolen it. The facts and feelings of the day moved across the screen in my head, as in a corny black-and-white movie where headlines or theatre marquees drift by diagonally and overlapping, overwhelming—Willy had taken my car in for work; Willy's voice sounded too concerned when I told him the GPS was stolen; Willy asked me how much the GPS originally cost; Mike, my mechanic, hadn't seen the GPS at all; this sort of thing doesn't happen in Vermont; I trust Mike completely. I woke up. It had to have been Willy. And then, when a little more awake, I could say something to myself that would put a black rubber stamp on all the drifting messages: he must have used it to buy drugs. Fuck.

I "knew" it was Willy before I'd gone to bed, but I hadn't allowed all the pieces to fit together until the middle of the night, when swarming facts settled down in my beehive brain. After that night I started to refer to these times as experiences of "knowing while not knowing," the stuff of Freudian analysis, repression, denial, intellectualization, a dozen defense mechanisms all specifying ways in which a person fools herself. Protects herself. Fools and protects. It became clear that the only way I could get through the day and continue working, making dinners, and being with friends was to not know what I knew. I pride myself on being able to always predict the next big scare in any horror movie, to anticipate the cliché climax in a drama when the lead character will reveal her abusive childhood, to know as I did when watching *The Crying Game* that the prostitute was transgender, way before we all even knew what transgender meant, knowing it so clearly that I had to ask Paul at the end of the movie, "So, what was the big surprise people were talking about?" But this was one thing I could not let myself know. Paul is my husband and the person whom I need to protect from surprise while watching horror movies, anticipating for him that a big scare is about to come, so that he doesn't scream out loud. It is my role as wife and mother to anticipate. But I needed to admit to myself that here I was dumb. Foggy. Perhaps this is what it is like to slowly develop Alzheimer's and believe you are thinking as you normally think, tightly and densely figuring things out, when, in reality, your thinking has pockets of air in it, big, empty pockets. So I woke Paul up, or thought I did since he was already awake, and shared that it was Willy who'd stolen the GPS. "That's what I thought," he said, "but I didn't want to say."

PART II

Addiction

1. ADDICTS

On TV and in the movies, addicts look desperate, antsy, agitated, crawling out of their skin. It may be overacting. Or it may be that they are poor addicts who have had to wait too long for their next fix instead of addicts from more privileged families who may think, look, and act more normally. Addicts from richer families can sit quietly and wait for the right moment, fitting in with family life, conversing, laughing, jollying their little brother out of a bad mood. They wait for you to go upstairs to take your shower, till they hear the click of the bathroom door, the clunk before the shower spray. That is enough time to walk down the hall to the front desk, take out a wallet from a bulging black purse, the kind mothers carry and that contains Band-Aids, Tylenol, chocolate, a tweezer, all potential necessities suggesting a preparedness that doesn't exist. Once the wallet is out, it's important to assess how much money is in there and what won't be missed, one out of six twenties for example, one five out of six fives. If there is only one twenty, the wallet is returned unchanged, and a new plan is hatched.

The mothers of addicts will know what I'm talking about when I say that we never really knew if our sons were on drugs or not. The son who chatted with us, looked us in the eye, sat down for a cup of coffee to have a talk could have been high the same way that the son who fell asleep on the couch and growled at us to leave him alone when we tried to make him go upstairs to sleep in his bed was—he could have been high, or not. I knew the first time Willy got high, his sophomore year of high school, when he came home from trick-or-treating with a bunch of boys from school. But that was all right, wasn't it? It was weed and inevitable that a fifteen-year-old would smoke. I suspected him of being high other times during his high school years. But I dealt with it—Paul and I dealt with it—by nagging, suspecting, complaining, fighting, grounding him, and then still letting him go, to sleepovers, to college, to study abroad, even to his own apartment. Letting him go. Later I realized I should have kept him at home, always, every night. I shouldn't have let him go to college.

Why didn't I grasp the seriousness of Willy's drug use? I'd like to say that in the last year of his addiction there was something different about him, but it seemed like more of the same, and so the depth of his addiction wasn't clear. Not to us. Not even to Willy's therapist.

Paul and I confronted Willy, many times, helpless parents outside his bedroom, a boundary that was sometimes difficult to cross. We were disappointed in him. We wanted to understand. We had questions. It was only weed, right? Pot. How long? When? Where? He could always end a confrontation by hiding in himself, simply not speaking. What could he say to us? He was caught. Did we ground him? Probably. What difference did grounding ever make?

Paul and I are at the Twisted Monkey listening to Willy's band, the oldest people in the bar, and I am sure it is as if there is a neon sign above us flashing "parents." Willy is the only one on the stage, with two beer bottles next to him, and he is taking a swig between every song. Paul is worried about the drinking, but I wrongfully dismiss him—Paul worries about everything. I think to myself, This is normal. I drank beer in college. Who didn't? I drank a lot when I worked in bars in graduate school. That's what kids do.

Willy could always hide from us, in broad daylight. He preferred this to lying, but there was lying too. Now all of our memories are under suspicion, from the beginning of the drug use to the end. If I bring them into the light and turn them this way and that, they may end up in a whole other narrative than the one in which they were first featured. Life continues as a family sitcom until it is jerked into a cop show, then, in the middle of the night, in one's worst nightmare, a tragedy.

2. THE MMPI-2

The 567 True/False items on the MMPI-2 sum up the personalities of the parents I evaluate, and they do this in ways that lawyers like. The Minnesota Multiphasic Personality Inventory. If a client can get through all 567 statements, written for those with at least a sixth-grade reading level, then he or she can be summarized diagnostically. Perhaps more importantly, there are scales that will indicate whether the client is lying. Not just lying but showing a whole array of test-taking attitudes that color the results.

There are the traditional validity scales, called the Lie Scale and the Fake Bad Scale (now known as the Symptom Validity Scale), joined by the Variable Response Inconsistency Scale, which tells you if someone has a seriously strange preference for selecting True or False, and one more that catches the random filling-in of the True and False circles just for the fun of it. The Lie Scale indicates that the client is representing himself in too glowing a light. He chooses False for a number of items that the vast majority of us would choose True for, or vice versa. These items, that are like "I have sometimes thought of stealing an item from a store" or "I have never had trouble working a remote control to get Netflix" catch him trying to slant the results positively.

The parents whom I evaluate mostly receive high scores on the Lie Scale, making the results hard to use in court. Sometimes a Fake Bad parent appears. The Fake Bad Scale has come under some controversy as it has been shown to incorrectly label psychiatric patients, women in particular, as embellishers and malingerers. In those cases, rarely is the mom faking so much as she is sending out a cry for help. In taking the test, she focuses on every pain, every moment of suffering, answering True so liberally she is almost off the charts. It may be puzzling to some people to think that parents who want their children returned to them truthfully report each and every symptom. But people want to be known, fully known, and the attraction of these 567 items is that they promise to tell all to them as well as to me.

The MMPI has gone through a few revisions to correct for the outdated wording of items. The original test items were chosen with little consideration of content and based on the percentage endorsed by the good people of Minnesota or psychiatric patients. These items, while thus statistically validated, were sometimes oddly related to the clinical diagnosis. If the original Minnesotans who were depressed endorsed an item like "I love pork chops" in greater numbers than those from the normal group, "I love pork chops" became an item on the D Is for Depression Scale.

The odd original comparison sample is referred to as "Minnesota Normal," because back in the 1940s, when the test was first developed, psychiatrists used mostly white skilled laborers and farmers who were visiting the psychiatric hospital, "normal" people compared to the inpatients. The test has been revised, and today's MMPI-2 is arguably the most frequently used psychological test in a forensic setting.

The "MMPI-RF" (revised form) is available as an alternative to the MMPI-2 and was created to address some problems of the original. The RF differentiates between depressed, called "emotional/internalizing dysfunction," and demoralized, called "demoralization." It might be important to distinguish between these two in our pill-happy society, with psychiatrists ready to overdiagnose depression among those suffering from loss, poverty, joblessness, stress, and discrimination, and especially among those whose children are in foster care and are trying to meet the demands from DCF.

True or False: "I wake up sad every morning." Most parents who have recently lost a child will say True.

True or False: "I cry more than I used to." If your child is in foster care, you cry more than you used to.

True or False: "I find myself resenting people." If you have been battling DCF, you find yourself resenting people.

True or False: "The world is stacked against me." "I worry that things will not turn out okay for me." If you have been to your DCF hearings, you might get those impressions.

Those items, which I have invented so as not to reveal secrets of the profession that I am sworn to keep, could contribute to a final diagnosis of depression or anxiety or paranoia or sometimes to the label "psychopathic deviate." But I rarely find these diagnoses accurate.

So why do I and others use the MMPI? The Daubert Standard states that an expert must use evidence that has been scientifically proven and tested. Has the theory or technique been tested, subject to peer review, and publication? Is there a known error rate? Are there standards controlling the use of this theory or technique? And, according to *Frye v. the United States*, has it attracted widespread acceptance within a relevant scientific community?

The MMPI-2, renormed in the 1980s using a diverse group of people, has just the scientific validity the courts want. My clinical judgment? Not so much. In writing a report, I have to add my clinical opinion to the MMPI to interpret it correctly. That's the catch-22 of using so many of these empirically based instruments. The science is good, but the science applies to groups. A group of people who were shown to be depressed by other instruments and interviews was also found to score high on this particular pattern of symptoms called the Depression Scale. Even the creators of the instrument don't want you to use that scale alone to diagnose depression. They ask that clinicians use their clinical judgment, their *unscientific* expertise, to interpret these findings in combination with other findings from other instruments.

So, in court, I offer something and then take it back. I give a diagnosis and then pull a rug out from under it. I present the science and accompany it with an interpretation. Sometimes I use the interpretive summary the MMPI-2 people offer, a beautifully written summary that is crushing in its exacting description if it is you who are being described. I have seen parts of these summaries cut and pasted verbatim into other psychologists' reports, without quotation marks, lifted whole. The more I read the computer-generated summaries, the more easily I can figure out which item leads to which output sentences in the report, which item triggers a sentence that's a jab at someone's parenting. I quote the computer sparingly and add my own words as cushion.

Addicts don't fare well on these tests. The diagnoses, syndromes, and their interpretations can be used in such a way as to provide a reasonable view of most people, but for former addicts, it's a losing battle. They almost always come out as "psychopathic deviates." It's not only the MMPI-2 that leads to this; on similar instruments, like the Millon Multi-Axial Clinical Inventory-4, addicts tend to be deemed "sociopaths." Is every addict a sociopath? Of course not. But has every addict lied, stolen, used drugs, and hurt the people he or she loved in careless and selfish ways? Very likely. Have many been underachievers? If they started their drug use in high school or earlier, yes, probably. Have their family relationships in the past been stormy? For certain. There is, however, no syndrome called "temporary sociopathy."

This overreach comes from the way the items are worded—have you "ever"? Or "in the past did you?" There is no item they can endorse that states, "In the past I was lost but now I'm found." The tests are predicated on the underlying assumption that people don't change and on the underlying belief that addiction can't happen to just any of us. *Sociopath. Psychopathic deviate.* Powerful words. When a psychologist writes these words in a report, they will glow supernaturally, beckoning the opposing counsel. I wonder how many lawyers have seen the label "sociopath" on a report, unqualified, uninterpreted, and unexplained, and went for the jugular with the parent on the stand. What judge would return a child to a deviate? Not any judge I know.

3. A MOTHER'S RELAPSE

A mother gets out of jail and assumes she will get her child back. It has only been twelve months. She has lain on her stiff mattress looking at photos of her child taped to the cinderblocks, dreaming of this reunification, finding a cozy apartment, making her child breakfast, moving alphabet letters around on the fridge—she will take her to Disneyworld! These dreams may have helped her get sober in jail, where individual and group therapy are provided, along with AA and NA meetings, every day. Inmates go to these because they are required to, or because there is nothing better to do, or because this time they really are going to get sober, and they attend even when there are drugs in jail to be had, as everyone knows.

The DCF worker is unsure whether this mother is ready to parent, and after one, two, or even three years in jail, is she? Her child is in such a lovely foster home, one with a big sister, two parents, two golden retrievers and an old beagle, a foster home that could become pre-adoptive, and then adoptive, a home that will someday nurture her child through a shaky adolescence and get her into college, and support her when she drops out for a semester or a year to find herself, and will permit her a visit with her biological father when he gets out of jail, because she should know him, shouldn't she, if only to meet him and ask him questions, and then not allow another visit because it upsets her, but allow his mother, the child's grandmother, to continue to stop by and bring Easter baskets and Christmas presents. I can't help but think that, because of all this, this mother hasn't got a chance. This foster family is stable enough to allow into their lives the chaos of the child's biological family now and again and still hold her tightly in their steady embrace through the confusion.

My inclination in making recommendations is to protect stability so that a child can thrive. Children don't like change, so if they are to be moved, it should be the last move. If I am evaluating whether a child should be returned to her mother after a lengthy jail sentence, I try to understand what stability the mother has set up in her life outside prison, mindful that she most likely hasn't had a lot of time to do so. And I try to assess the self-knowledge gained through all kinds of therapy she received while in jail, because that self-knowledge will play a part in preventing a relapse. Or if she does relapse, it will encourage her to seek out help and make the relapse a short one.

Relapses are typical in all sorts of disorders that require behavior change. It is now common knowledge (and our parenting coach informed us) that in battling obesity, nicotine addiction, and the behaviors that contribute to diabetes and heart disease, one can expect seven to nine relapses before reaching the equivalent of sobriety. I remind myself of this often, and I tell my students this, too, when they face the disappointment of a counseling client's relapse. Clients are taught in self-help programs from Weight Watchers to AA, to minimize slip-ups—one piece of pie does not ruin the whole diet; back in the saddle tomorrow; one day at a time. The road towards sobriety is not an expressway. It's a city street with stops and starts. But when an addict is in recovery, relapses become shorter and spaced further apart over time. Even with the knowledge that relapsing is a normal part of recovery, depending on when it occurs, just a single relapse can result in a child's return to foster care, which may then become for the child, a pre-adoptive home. When a child has been in custody for one or two years, there is no time to spare to support a mother's meandering path to sobriety. If she wants her child back, she will simply do what most addicts cannot do—just stop.

I ask this mother, Gloria, "Why was Jessie taken from your care?" Gloria is all smiles and perkiness, sitting on my couch in my office, her hand resting over the worn bit, playing with the threads, and making me feel bad for being too cheap to get professional-looking furniture and keeping the flowered couch that was a hand-me-down from the therapist who previously used this office. Gloria looks as if she believes her smiles can reassure me, as if she has had a history of smiling over lies. I'm not immune to pretty smiles. I smile a therapist's smile back, friendly, even warm, but unrevealing.

"It was a mistake the second time," replies Gloria, starting in on the second time and smiling past the first. The second time DCF took her child? The second relapse? Gloria tells me a story about how DCF made a mistake and thought she was being abused by a man who was sleeping in her home. She argued that she wasn't, but her child was taken into custody for a short time until the man no longer lived there. I check the notes I took from the case disposition sent to me by the DCF social worker.

The third time, say the notes, a neighbor reported that little Jessica had toddled out of the apartment and down the stairs and was sitting alone in the driveway to the building's parking lot. I read that part aloud to her. "That was someone else's child," Gloria stated. Gloria's slight tone of annoyance indicated that she thought that DCF had gotten it all wrong, that these weren't good and accurate reasons to remove a child. I have seen errors in DCF histories, and I've repeated these in my reports, unwittingly. Still, the idea that they got this fact so wrong seemed difficult to believe.

We were not yet talking about Gloria's addiction. We had been talking around the effects of addiction on her life, and I could look down the road a bit and see the end of it: Gloria would be letting me know that even when she was high, she was a good mother. "I take it you think DCF shouldn't have removed Jessica?" I ask. Gloria pauses and then tells me about when DCF first became involved. "My mother told on me to DCF." Her mother reported that Gloria had track marks on her arms. That was true, Gloria admitted, but she argued that her mother should have talked to her first about the track marks because her mother would have then realized it was "just experimentation" and that DCF didn't have to get involved.

That word "just." It irritates me. When I taught undergraduates and gave them a complex final writing assignment, they would often reflect back to me, "So you just want us to . . . ?" I know that they wanted me to reduce the assignment to a just this or just that in order to relieve their anxiety about it, make it seem more manageable, but I felt cornered by them, pushed into agreeing to a "just" when there were many different parts of the assignment to be worked out. So I would say, "No, it isn't 'just' that. It's also this." And they would reply, "So it's just that and this."

"Just experimenting" with heroin, says a mother of a baby, a baby on her lap, on the couch with her, in the room next door, a baby she is taking care of. All right, then, let's move on to the abuse by the man who was sleeping on her couch. "What about that man on the couch?

I read in the DCF disposition that there were injuries a neighbor re-ported? He hurt you?" Gloria responds that DCF was stupid for be-lieving that neighbor. She, Gloria, knows whether she was abused or not. I hear about vindictive neighbors a lot. I can believe it, when I'm sitting there in my office listening empathically. But on the whole, could this world be full of so many vindictive neighbors?

I feel my body in its big armchair across from the flowered couch jerk back to a corner of the room as if on a Tilt-a-Whirl. I look at her from afar for a minute and think, What was the guy doing on her couch anyway? I get tired of hearing about homes with children in them where anyone is allowed to spend the night on the couch, stay a week, or a month, for a few dollars, to hide out, to sell drugs. One could assume that in the current economy, this is the generosity of the poor towards other poor. It sometimes is. But I venture a guess with Gloria, "Was the guy on the couch an addict?" and she answers, "Yes." And when I ask her why she would allow someone addicted to drugs to sleep on her couch when she was taking care of a baby, she replies that she is a compassionate person, a person who likes to take care of other people. I remind Gloria that in a previous ruling the judge had ordered her not to allow drug users in her home. Why did she do that anyway, given the risk, given what the judge ordered?

"I don't really understand myself sometimes," she answers, per-haps for the first time, truthfully.

I weigh the prevention of loss against opportunity in an adop-tive home. I weigh motherlove against the stability the foster home provides Gloria's daughter. I think her daughter should remain with her foster family.

But I also ask myself, What kind of stability did I provide? and I discover it's a very hard question to answer. We had to move when Willy was eleven, before fifth grade, away from his best friend Davey and Davey's family, which had been like having cousins just a block away. This was the end of a period of bliss in which Willy and Davey spent every day after school together, bundled up in a recliner in front of the TV, unaware that in one year's time they would be older boys who could no longer cuddle like that again for years, if ever. They swung on backyard swings, designed races on skateboards down the hilly part of the street, concocted potions in the kitchen.

We had to move when I didn't get tenure at Bryn Mawr College, what was for a time the great shame of my life, although others who don't obtain tenure seem to recover more quickly. I sat for a year like a zombie in front of the TV, and Paul took a job in Michigan in case I couldn't find work. That year of job hunting consolidated my suspicion that my upbringing in apartment buildings and playing in back alleys and empty lots meant that I would never be able to have a foundation among old stone buildings and those phony "traditions." Bryn Mawr was a place of privileged private-schooled girls, one of whom wrote on my course evaluations, "The professor was very available but not available when I wanted her to be." At those prices, one needed to feed-on-demand. I also interpreted my tenure denial as, in part, revenge for the times I didn't hold my tongue. I said the wrong thing or looked critically at the chair's beginning affair with a student. I was and still am hard to censor, afraid of wealthy people, critical to a fault, never a suck-up, always the one who wanted to be smarter, wanting more than anything to be seen as smart rather than nice, when my life-long lesson to be learned was that all that matters is being smart enough and very, very nice. I should have sucked it up for my children, to be able to ward off a crisis, for stability's sake. But I couldn't. I relapsed time and again.

4. A MOTHER IN PRECONTEMPLATION

The call was from attorney Sandra Morris, whom I hadn't heard from for a few years, since she asked me to speak to the court generally about why children make false reports of sexual abuse. I am very comfortable speaking about the research on false and true reporting among children. In that particular case, one woman, let's call her Mary, had returned to her Christian fundamentalist church with her daughter and renounced her sexual orientation and her past with the girl's other mother, Mary's former partner, whom I'll call Annie. Annie had not carried the child but had planned the child with

Mary—which counts in my book. They had arranged for and carried out the alternative insemination together and had always been co-parents. Annie wanted visits with the child after she and Mary split up, but Mary's church believed that allowing this six-year-old girl to visit her lesbian parent in Vermont was akin to sending her on a visit to a brothel. Generally, I don't like to give testimony against children in order to protect grown-ups who may or may not be wrongly accused. I feel so unsure of being in the right and generally want to be the one who speaks on behalf of children who can't speak for themselves. But in this case, I was only asked to look at the evidence on paper and present research I could find on false reports and coaching, that is, what kinds of statements do children make that seem to be consistent with a false accusation.

Attorney Morris is quick and analytical, a formidable adversary when I am a witness for the victim and she is the lawyer for the perpetrator. I appreciate her and she me. She doesn't try to attack my expertise on the stand. Nor does she try to trap me into making a choice: "Shall I call you Sharon or Dr. Lamb?" If I say "Dr. Lamb," I'll sound haughty, which is not a great style for Vermont, and if I say "Sharon," I'll sound unprofessional. So I smile and apologetically say, "In the courtroom, I guess you can call me Dr. Lamb because I'm here in my professional capacity as a psychologist." I don't need to do that with Sandra because she'll trap me in some other way into saying something she'd like me to say.

Today on the phone she sounds like an advocate, concerned about a mother who has had a longstanding opiate addiction and is about to be "kicked out" of the Lapp Center, where mothers and their infants or toddlers can be together while mothers try to recover from substance abuse. Sandra is representing the mother, Donna, and, I can tell, likes her a lot. She wants to help Donna get the support she needs so that she can parent her children, but Donna keeps relapsing.

I let Sandra know that we are all learning quite a bit about addictions, and we need to take a less punishing attitude. This I've learned in my own life from Willy's relapses.

"Mom, I had a relapse."

"Are you okay?"

"Yes."

"Can you get back on track?"

"Yes." No. Today I wonder why these words didn't make me just drop everything and move to wherever he was living, live with him, follow him around until he was clean and sober. I know in some vague undigested way that that's not supposed to be what parents do. Not even with addicts. But maybe I should have done that. Why didn't I just take over his life then and there, put him on one of those toddler leashes I used to look at with disgust.

The answer is that it has to come from him. It has to be his idea, his wish to get clean, or it won't work. Whose theory is that? Where does it come from? Therapists? Addiction counselors? Fathers? Not mothers. Not from me.

I tell her that the average number of relapses for opiate abusers is seven to nine, and that it takes a while to get clean and stay clean. Donna seems to have an easy time getting clean. She has always seemed invested in treatment and is sure that this time it's going to work. She is, Sandra is arguing already on the phone, a "good mom" and knows how to take care of her children. She's likeable and smart. She's given up opiates a number of times, however, she keeps being drawn back. This is such a typical scenario. Is it the pattern of standard recovery or of repeated failure?

Defense attorneys have to tell me nice things about their clients, kind of like real estate agents promoting a place you might want to buy. But Sandra sounds sincere. I tell her that when an addict is clean, the cravings continue and that they are powerful and hard to resist. I speak from experience, from what my son has told me, from what his therapists and my therapist have told us. But when I have said this on the stand, opposing counsel objects and points out that I am not an expert on addictions. I am on the stand solely to speak to child development and attachment. I don't correct opposing counsel out loud but think: I am now an expert on addictions.

Donna is someone who's been struggling, who thinks she can do it but keeps having trouble. I want her to win. Because I already like her. Because she has older children to take care of and not just an infant. But also because I don't want anyone to say my son can't be a good father because of a relapse. The center wants Donna to leave because she is not "contemplative." Sandra wants to know, "What does that mean? 'Contemplative'?" I actually know what they are referring to. The therapist was speaking about the second stage of addiction recovery, according to a model developed by Carlo DiClemente and James Prochaska in 1984. This model has six stages. The first stage is "pre-contemplation" and refers to the period when addicts have not yet taken a good, hard look at the problems their addiction has caused them. They are in denial about the costs to themselves and others, and haven't really identified their addiction as a problem. They rationalize or feel stuck or are rebellious. They tend to think that others are overreacting.

In the "contemplation" stage, though, the person recognizes that a problem exists. She may not yet be able to make a commitment to change, but she knows that drugs have caused a problem in her life. I wonder, though, if whether or not a person with an addiction can contemplate the problems in her life depends on who's listening.

Sandra tells me that all four of Donna's children were born with Oxycontin in their system. A doctor had once prescribed Percocet for her sciatic nerve pain, even though he knew she was pregnant. Donna claims that she didn't know that a doctor would prescribe something that had the potential to harm her or her baby. In the beginning, she functioned well on it, even caring for her sick grandmother. After a while, though, she noticed a change, and all she could think about was getting high to ward off withdrawal symptoms.

Two of Donna's children are in foster care. One is home with her husband, and her new baby is with her at the Lapp Center. She may lose all of these children, even though she has appeared able to function well as a mother, even though her husband is not an addict. Why? Because, by all DCF accounts, he is hopeless as head of the household. He needs her management skills for the family to operate. Sandra tells me that DCF agrees; in spite of her addiction, Donna managed the home and cared for her children fairly well.

When Sandra says the number four, as in four children, I feel a dull disappointment. I no longer feel as if I can save Donna and help Sandra make the court see that addiction is a tough row to hoe or that Donna can't be fully blamed because she is struggling with a chronic illness, addiction. Four children. I silently ask myself something I've asked before: Why can't she just stop using?

I also wonder, Why hasn't she been in long-term therapy? Why hasn't she been on Suboxone replacement therapy? Why is she still in this pre-contemplation stage? How is she able to convince everyone that she is all right at certain times during her process of recovery? I am guessing she knows how to hide the addiction well.

I thank Sandra and tell her I will interview Donna. I will see if she fools me, too, fools me as I have been fooled before. My part in this particular family's story will be a small one. I am only to evaluate the mother and not the children. Can an addict be a good enough mother? Maybe. On paper. I'll see.

5. A CHILD IN THE GARDEN

Abbie needs to be in control. After waiting for some time now for her mother to get clean, she needs to be in charge. That's clear enough as she moves the grown-ups around the room, tugging at them to be in place for a game she has invented, then grabs the dog's leather collar and drags the rather large and somewhat resistant collie to his cushion. We let her, right now. He lets her. She is making a game of her need to control, and that's a very good thing. Later, when she is asked to cooperate with a task and refuses, growling like the dog, it's not as good. Growling like a dog is rarely a good sign in a child, even if she is only four. But if a child can work out her fears and needs and worries in a game, it will help her develop resources for life as its lived, and she may be able to cooperate with the simple requests her foster mother gives her.

I am doing an observation in a foster home. I am never there to evaluate the foster parents, who have already been evaluated by DCF, but to watch the child, Abbie, in a more natural environment and to compare her behavior in this home to her behavior during visits with her mother. Foster mothers in Vermont are almost always good enough mothers. They are responsive, reflect back feelings and thoughts to their charges, and encourage responsibility by asking them to contribute to small jobs around the house.

"Can you help me garden? Where's your hoe? Go get it and you can help me in the garden. Put on your gardening boots." Dark-haired Abbie, with the rosebud mouth and chubby cheeks, pulls on her rubber boots with butterflies on them, then gleefully runs to get the hoe, delighted with the opportunity to participate in a very important job. She sets the orange plastic hoe into the dirt by a blueberry bush and begins moving it back and forth in long lines that barely move a clump of dirt. I hear her saying, "Where is the mama snake? Where is Mama? Mama is hiding."

The foster mother tells me that Abbie is obsessed with a snake they had found the other day under a bush, along with her baby snakes. We don't have to explore the significance of this.

Now the gardening is over, and her foster father comes out, picks her up, gives her a hug, then rests her on the boney angle of his hip. Will she take the hug? I watch. First yes. She leans in. Then no. She leans away just a bit. I write this down on my pad. Now yes, she leans back in. She accepts the hug. He puts her down, and she runs to the place where the mama snake was.

Crouched by the hole where the snake was last found, the way toddlers can use their knees to support a full crouch, she yells to us that the snake isn't there. Then she runs to the faucet outside the house shouting, "Let's all wash our hands." We mosey over and allow Abbie to herd us into a line for washing. She washes her foster father's hands, then her foster mother's hands, then my hands after I lay down my pad of paper and pen in the grass. Then she washes her own hands. We're all together, washing our hands. This routine seems very satisfying.

Abbie's mother isn't ready for her child yet, but I want her to succeed. Debra is a super smart young woman of mixed race, which must have been unusual growing up in Vermont, where most of the parents and children I see are white. She also seems to have had more of a middle-class upbringing than most. She once volunteered at the library and is a reader who talks about the books she is currently reading. She has read about addiction too.

In the observation visit earlier that week at the DCF office, Debra was quite good with Abbie, letting her take the lead and guessing right about Abbie's feelings when she reflected her daughter's feelings back to her. She kept Abbie safe, stopping her from climbing on the furniture. She cuddled Abbie when Abbie let her. And she let her simply go on being when Abbie was occupied in play. Abbie brought toys to her and asked her mom to set up a train set. She lay back against her mother, relaxing deep into her comfy body when her mother read her a book. It was easy for me to see that Abbie loved her mother and that there was an attachment. She wasn't overexcited by the visit as some children are, dizzy with energy, not knowing which toy to bring over, unable to titrate how close or how far a space to create between their own bodies and their parents. This was a comfortable pair who had consistently and reliably had visits while Abbie was in foster care, visits that maintained their earlier relationship.

It is early spring, when mama snakes and baby snakes appear in gardens and sometimes inside of houses, when ants crawl on kitchen counters and mice return to the outdoors, a time when gardeners in Vermont shuffle their packs of seeds, guessing when it's not too early to lay them down. Spring for Abbie means that she has been away from her mother for nine months.

Back in October, when Abbie's mother was ready to go to rehab, finally ready, she detoxed and stopped using, knowing that after rehab, DCF would start reunification with Abbie. There was a two-week wait to get into rehab though. There often is, but most people think that when an addict decides she needs rehab, the doors just open and take her in. Two weeks doesn't seem like a long time to some of us, but it is a long time for an addict. I understand that. So although Debra had stopped using, she spent the two-week wait time using again.

"Why?" I asked. I am always an innocent once again with each new addict.

"There was a gap in my treatment," she replied using words a counselor might use. During this gap, she told me, she was "middle-manning" to help out her friends Jim and Judy, who really needed a fix. Debra was on Suboxone to help her with cravings before she got to rehab and that was, in her opinion, a good way to wait it out. But then she started this middle-manning thing to help her friends who were "not as ready" as she was, finding them heroin or Suboxone or whatever she could.

She said, "I only used three or four times during my relapse, and they were primarily snorts, not IV." Here was that Suboxone question again. Was she using it as a drug or as a way to stop cravings? Why was she calling this use a relapse?

"Why?" I asked, although I tell my students to reflect back feelings and thoughts to a client and not ask so many questions. If you want to know more, I advise them, say, "Tell me more." There is a less accusatory feel to that, as with the phrase, "I'm curious about . . ." But with Abbie's mother, I asked, "Why?" I wanted to know how it was that she couldn't see she was taking too many risks in those two weeks.

Debra explained that occasionally she could just snort the Suboxone to taste it, even though she didn't get the rush.

"Why?"

"Because of cravings."

"Looking back, do you think it was a little bit risky to your sobriety to be around dealers?"

"No."

"To be hanging out with friends who use?"

"No."

"Why? Why not?"

"Jim had nowhere else to go. I needed to help him get the—heroin."

There was something about this woman's intelligence that I had come to respect in our talks, but then, when talking about drugs,

heroin, Suboxone, her using, her relapse, her middle-manning—
what she said stopped making sense. Every time I asked why, her
answer implied that I should know the answer already, as if each
answer had a tag "of course" at the end. Could this be the kind of
thinking AA and NA talks about, the kind of thinking that addicts
do that just doesn't make sense to the sober? Stinkin' thinkin'? Here
she was saying that she had all the confidence in the world, after just
giving up opiates, that she could be around friends still using heroin,
work with dealers to procure heroin, handle the heroin, and still not
use heroin by snorting Suboxone. That's a lot of self-control. Or a hell
of a lot of denial.

I found myself as confused as I was when I spoke to the doctor
at Willy's first rehab, a man with a paternal Texas drawl but none of
the slang, except for a y'all or two. He told Paul and me, on different
phones in different rooms of the house, as if we were manning our
positions in a war that was about to begin, that Willy was taking
some time to go through withdrawal. Why so long?

"Wayull," the doctor explained, "he was snorting heroin every
day before he got here. That's going to take some time to get out of
his system."

"But Willy didn't use heroin, doctor. He used Oxycontin." The
doctor must be confusing Willy with someone else, I thought. There
are probably a lot of other kids there, in rehab, on heroin. Willy told
us he stopped before he got that far.

"Oh, yes. That's right," the doctor said, quieter. Pausing. "It still
takes time."

I quickly filled the silence that followed the doctor's recanting
with more questions. But when I got off the phone, I had that same
dizzying feeling of not knowing what was right or real. And like a lie
come clean in the middle of the night, I woke up and knew. The doctor must have realized in the middle of our conversation that Willy
had never told us he had moved on to snorting heroin; the doctor had
just unwittingly breached confidentiality. My denial was not his to
break through.

Having concluded that when Debra said she'd relapsed she didn't mean the times she took Suboxone, I asked her, "Do you think that a part of you was planning to relapse?" When we work with people with addictions, sometimes we have to hold on to just a part of them that wants to do better, the smallest piece. We call it "part" language. In this case I was segregating the part that still wants to use, holding it at arm's length from the part of her that wanted to be clean.

"I don't think so," Debra said.

And to her credit, after that relapse, she got rid of her cell phone with all the numbers of dealers and drug-using friends in it. So she knew, or a part of her knew, that there was something wrong with keeping those connections, even if she couldn't quite conceptualize that for me in retrospect. Cell phones are lifelines for everyone these days but especially for addicts, who can reach dozens of potential dealers when they need to, texting, "What do you have?"

When I met with her, I tried to put together a chronology of her substance use, a task that I always find near to impossible to do.

"What happened after your first rehab then?" I asked.

"There wasn't wraparound." I knew what "wraparound" meant: a mental health treatment term that refers to the way services are provided. Just as it sounds, the treatment wraps the client with several kinds of services so there are no empty days or unmet needs.

"I only saw a counselor three times in twelve days," she said. "I wanted more. I needed more."

"So how did you handle that?"

"I thought, The system is failing me, but I'd better make the most of it. I was 'high risk.'"

And she relapsed. Again.

And then she had Abbie and was clean until Abbie was three months old.

"Why?"

"I don't know. Maybe because my friends were using?" Debra added, "I felt like I was a better mom when using."

Then a friend reported her to DCF for using.

She was angry at her friend and said, "She should have handled it differently."

I asked, "Why?"

"Because DCF takes your children."

"Maybe she was worried about Abbie's safety," I suggested.

She rolled her eyes. After Abbie was removed from her home, Debra had one last hurrah, and then another, promising herself she would get clean afterward.

She is in a sober house now and tells me she is committed to her program. She tells me she is different from the others there, more ready, more capable. In this halfway house she is better, she says, than "the rehab girls" who are mandated to be there and who give you a hard time if you actually want to change. I don't know whether to trust this comparison.

Responsibility is different from control. I hear Debra using the language of addiction treatment, but I hear her using it to blame everyone but herself. She had to wait too long for admission into a rehab. There wasn't wraparound when she left it. There wasn't enough counseling. Her friend should have done something different, shouldn't have called DCF. All this might be true, and I am inclined to blame the system here and there as well. But she planned a last hurrah. Planned it.

I also hear a sense of pride as she describes her recovery, her management, her current control. She asked to go to rehab. Asked. She is different from the girls who don't want to change, she says. Different. I try to put this all together, herding these positive facts like Abbie herds grownups.

Everyone has some sort of illusion of control, of other people or of themselves. Whether it's moving the people you love to the right places in the garden to keep your eye on them, to keep them safe, or it's putting yourself in situations with friends, pretending that you don't do, won't do drugs again. Maybe these illusions are good, keeping us hopeful and confident, feeling on top of things. But there is probably a good reason that the first step in AA is, We admitted we were powerless—that our lives had become unmanageable. In Al-Anon I am always working on the first step: we admitted we were powerless. But aren't we all?

6. REHAB SHOPPING

First comes detox and then comes rehab. I didn't know this back in 2010 when we sent Willy to the Brattleboro Retreat and he was discharged unexpectedly after three days. We had brought him there, thin, sick, and ashamed, not knowing it was a detox center, which is different from a rehab center. There he got medication to ease withdrawal while he smoked cigarettes non-stop in the clinic yard with other addicts who bragged about their binges and relapses and the several rehabs they had been to. Detoxing begins with giving a patient a substitute for his drug of choice, that mimics the effects of the drug, and then weaning him off of it, to hopefully put an end to all cravings. Doctors monitor the withdrawal symptoms, some of which—seizures, for example—can be very severe. We were surprised there was no therapy at this place, just psychopharmacology for detoxing. So began the search for a rehab center.

Vermont rehabs seemed at the time to me to not be an option. I associated these places with the women and men I evaluated, who never got better, even when they might lose their children. I know now that a high relapse rate is a problem in all rehab centers, not just the ones in Vermont. It's hard to confess, but I also imagined in these places low-income, white, and uneducated people, like my own family of origin. I don't glorify what it was like to grow up poor and have only potatoes to eat one week, hearing the constant fighting about money; I don't buy into the idea that this inevitably produces kids with "grit." Yes, there was the freedom of wandering back alleys and abandoned lots with multi-aged groups of kids. But there was also the visiting cousin of a neighbor from the Ozarks who tried to choke my sister to death while I beat on her back with my little six-year-old fists. And there was a neighborhood bully who would threaten to kill me behind the Kroger whenever she saw me, whispering those menacing words in my ear when she could get close enough and no one else could hear. And there was the sexual abuse, from my good friend Claudia's teen brother, who swooped each one of us up, and carried us to his cellar to stick his hand down our pants, until the neighborhood mothers caught on and put a stop to it. Of the three of these, the threat about Kroger was the most traumatic. This doesn't mean our parents weren't hardworking or worthy of admiration. But thank God for the suburban middle-class existence that began in third grade in Evanston, Illinois, a vast improvement. My dad used to say, "I've been poor and I've been well off, and I prefer being well off." As a tenured professor, I was certainly "well off," so I looked into private rehab centers for my son.

Buying a stint in a rehab is like buying a new car. There are salesmen and women who sound like they care. They sell options and accessories, and have better or worse deals. You have to haggle with them, but who would know that at the start? Not those who believe that health care is a right.

One center in Boston told me that Willy would have to wait months unless he entered through the emergency room, high and in need. "You mean, we would have to get him high again to get him into your program?" She answered, "I can't say that, but some parents have done that and it has worked." I considered that for a hot minute, but no. What would that mean to Willy?

I turned to the internet. If you just sniff at a rehab ad on the internet, new ads will follow you across your virtual journey no matter if you're visiting Nordstrom Rack or investigating the Paleo diet. Like a worry in the middle of the night, it follows neural roads into each of your next thoughts until you are awake and looking for *Law and Order* on TV.

It is almost impossible to determine what's a sham organization and what's an authentic center, even if one were foolish enough to believe there was a wide separation between the two. Some ads look like promises of health care and some look like promotions for a

Carnival cruise. They often draw you in with a narrative that makes a mother feel heard. They are all so kind to parents, nonjudgmental. Click on one, and you can chat with someone like Jill.

In our fifteen minutes together, Jill came to know everything about me and my family, including our insurance benefits. I was slow to understand that she wasn't representing a rehab center at all but a placement service that finds rehabs for callers, a place that quite certainly gets kickbacks. I discovered that many of the ads I was looking at were not actually for rehab centers themselves but for the brokers who received a fee for matching a client to a center.

Jill hooked me up to the first real salesman I spoke to—Mickey. Mickey worked for Brighter Tomorrow, or New Dawn, or Choices, or some such promisingly named rehab. None are called Underworld or Vacation from Life. Mickey was a recovering meth addict, comforting and charming. He had been to rehab himself, which gave me hope. As I told him about Willy, he made sarcastic comments, the way AA members tend to do, chuckling and sympathetic at the same time. He was the first person to tell me that joke about how do you know an addict is lying. He is speaking. I found that a bit harsh, at the time. This center was on Lake Michigan, reminding me of the cheap summer resort my father took us to one rare vacation. There was a dock at the resort and a twisting slide into the water, cabins, Kool-Aid we called bug juice, and two teenage female counselors among many I was obsessed with who suffered my adulation and were kind to me when I couldn't form a tight lanyard.

I bonded with Mickey, who answered so many of my initial questions about addiction. "That's a good sign," he said when I told him that Willy had been trying to get clean on his own. "The only normal people are the ones I don't know," Mickey told me. "One day at a time." There would be more meaningful slogans to come. I mistook his warmth and familiarity to be the style of the rehab instead of the style of the salespeople who spoke with more than a soupçon of AA. "My wife drives this same car" was a typical approach from salesmen that I learned when I was looking to buy a new car. In my search for a rehab, this was transformed into "My cousin went through the three-month program."

When Mickey started pressuring me to sign up at the end of that phone call, I distanced myself from him, stopped asking questions and eliciting information about services I wasn't going to pay for. He quoted me $35,000 for three months. "Insurance pays for this, right?" I foolishly asked. Another foolish question I asked was "What is your success rate?" He hesitated.

As I later learned, there is no accurate success rate for any of these rehabs because the majority of drug addicts relapse before they are clean "for good," no matter if they have been to rehab or not. Sure, 80 percent of the residents may leave a place clean and sober. But if they don't contact the rehab once they've relapsed, the rehabs don't have the information to change their statistics. The truth is that there are no promises. Sometimes a rehab can give the addict a good start that he can make use of out in the real world, but many come back or try a different rehab.

The next person I spoke to was Delia, who was no-nonsense and wasn't going to waste her time with me if I wasn't going to pay. She asked me about insurance right away and said she would call me back to have a discussion about the rehab program. What Delia did while I waited was figure out how much of the rehab my insurance would pay for. Insurance companies don't typically pay for inpatient rehab centers, but the centers can bill for some of the treatment they provide. For example, because a psychiatrist was on staff, they could charge for his treatment, and the money would go to the rehab, which pays the psychiatrist. If insurance pays for one or two therapy appointments a week in intensive outpatient rehab, it pays for the same inside. Insurance doesn't pay for room and board, though, because there is little research that shows that inpatient treatment is any more effective than intensive outpatient. The research does not take into account a parent's perspective that a child is less likely to die while locked in a rehab center than when free outside of it. That fact needs no research.

When Delia called back, her voice was a tad softer and more persuasive. I knew my insurance must be good. She started describing that the center used the most up-to-date strategies—evidence-based. They used a twelve-step model and added onto that motivational interviewing, family treatment, skills training, vocational counseling, and a full physical therapy program. They were also "dual diagnosis," which means they served those who were not only addicted but who also had an underlying mental illness such as anxiety, depression, or bipolar disorder. I do not believe that anxiety and depression experienced prior to addiction can be separated from anxiety and depression experienced during or because of addiction, and so most addicts get a dual diagnosis. I suppose that from the point of view of rehabs, which is about getting the most out of insurance companies, this is a good thing. The recommendation was three or four months at $20,000 a month.

There was one rehab that was for musicians and had a recording studio. That one was $35,000 a month. Three months and I could have bought Willy his own recording studio. I got the quote and got off the phone.

Then there was plain-spoken Margaret, who worked at a rehab center in Iowa that proudly did not use the AA model but rather, she bragged, evidence-based cognitive-behavior therapy. I know the claims of the evidence-based psychotherapy movement and the problematic research designs that have led to claims that some psychotherapy models do better than others. But Margaret appealed to me because she didn't use the language of illness. Willy just had wrong ways of looking at things. AA calls it "stinkin' thinkin'," but don't tell that to Margaret. This was the cheapest rehab because they moved the men to sober-living houses quickly, and from these houses the men attended classes all day and perhaps in the evening too. But imagining Willy walking the cold dirty streets of an Iowa city gave me the chills. I saw rundown buildings and alleyways in failing neighborhoods. I don't know why. I may have been picturing a film about Detroit.

So, not till after I spoke to Mickey, nor after I heard from Delia, nor after the third phone call from Margaret, nor after several more phone calls to California and Florida rehabs, but after each and every one had called back with different and better financial offers than their first ones, did I understand I had to haggle.

Of the three recommendations on Dr. Phil's website, I called a center that was pretty much the farthest from Vermont, the one in Texas. The salesman, Brian, was, again, a former addict. He seemed to be willing to make deals more quickly and more straightforwardly than the others. I was quick now at naming a price we would be able to manage, and Brian was quick to respond by taking down the insurance information and seeing what he could and couldn't offer for that price. He sold me on the "extras," which was a similar experience to when I bought the tailgate spoiler that juts off the roof at the back of my Honda CRV, a little something that got thrown in at the last minute as the car dealer and I talked price. Brian said everyone gets, free of charge, an "awesome" follow-up service for the first year after discharge through a support network called MAP. This turned out to be a cowboy-talking guitarist named Ernie. Brian also answered honestly about relapse, saying that it was difficult to talk about success rates but that 75 percent finish the program and are clean when they leave. That seemed honest.

I was concerned about the conservativeness of Texas, and I told Brian that we were Democrats, we came from Vermont, were Jewish, and had many gay friends and relatives. We were worried about what it would be like for Willy there. He told me he was a Democrat too. I found out later, however, that he thought that I was speaking code for Willy being gay, and he had written down in his notes that Willy was gay when he wasn't. When Paul and I later got the intake notes to assist us in a lawsuit against our health insurance company, I was surprised to read the staff had interpreted Willy's behaviors through a homophobic lens. They saw him as inappropriately making advances to the other guys there and told him he couldn't wear his short shorts any more, shorts we admittedly had also identified as "kind of gay" back in Vermont.

The days at home with an addict who at that point wants to go into rehab are tense. Willy could disappear in an instant. He looked online at the options I'd found for him and liked the Texas one best. Of course, Malibu Wonderland wasn't on the list. But the deal I was offered by Brian was one I wasn't entirely comfortable with. To be able to work with the $20,000 we were offering, he said that Willy would get two months in the center and one month in the halfway house but that this halfway house was fully monitored and its clients are invited over to the big house for therapy and other meetings.

There was one minor glitch that occurred after we made our down payment and got Willy ready to fly to Texas. Looking over the email exchange with Brian, I scrolled down past the latest message to earlier ones. Brian had accidentally forwarded an email from the owner of the rehab congratulating him on "hooking me" and saying I was a "tough one" to nail. I brought this to Brian's attention and also to the owner's. They both apologized. But by that time I knew that rehab is big business, and so the language was no surprise. I suppose I took it as a compliment.

7. LYING

In my forensic work, I've been fooled, lied to, tricked, and manipulated by parents. Parents leave out bits of their stories that will make them look bad for the evaluation. Those who admit to bad deeds produce excuses and distortions of the truth. A few times, I've given myself heart and soul to a mother sitting across from me only to understand later that I've been lied to.

There are different kinds of lies. There are the misrepresentations of anyone who's trying to hide an addiction or sugarcoat their past. If they have been to AA, I can recognize the AA voice of oversharing, which is supposed to sound like someone taking responsibility. When I don't hear that, I assume that the facts will be manipulated in an attempt to avoid the shame.

Some lies are obvious, but I can handle those. I sit in front of the lying parent with the printed DCF case plan in front of me, reading the facts. I do this after the mother has given me her story.

"Okay, I'm reading here—what about the time DCF says you slapped your daughter?"

"No, that never happened."

"It says here that DCF learned about this from a friend of yours."

"She's lying. She wanted to sleep with my husband. We're not friends anymore."

"Okay. But it says here your daughter told the social worker it happened."

"She learned to lie from her father."

There have been a few pathologically lying dads whose bragging about lives of danger and foreign travel raised red flags.

"DCF says that they checked some register and you were never a Navy SEAL."

"It was classified, so how could they have checked?"

"Well, they say here you gave them your platoon number and it didn't exist."

"They must have checked under my current name. I used a different name when I enlisted."

"But you didn't give that name to DCF? Why not?"

"I don't like to talk about it. I killed about twenty people, innocent and not. I'll bring in the papers next time I see you."

Needless to say, the dad kept forgetting to bring me the papers. And when I visited his trailer to do a home observation with his daughter and asked to see the papers then, darn if they weren't at his mother's house in North Carolina.

There are also retractions. A retraction is when someone says the truth at first and then in a subsequent meeting takes it back, or vice versa. I didn't know what to make of George's retraction. George was a sex offender who had served his time in prison and completed three years of group therapy for sex-offending men, having admitted to what he did. He had sexually abused a twelve-year-old girl, the daughter of a girlfriend who took off and left her daughter in his care. She became a sort of partner to George, helping him to raise his own five-year-old child. Was he lying three years ago when he admitted he had sexually abused the girl? Or was he lying now when he told me that three years ago he said what he needed to say in order to be able to have supervised visits with his daughter? He and his daughter, now eight, have developed a wonderful relationship through his two-hour-a-week supervised visits that had been going on since he was released from jail.

I called on a psychologist I know who regularly tests sex offenders and who tested George three years ago and again more recently. "George? Yeah, I just saw him. He's got a new girlfriend, his own age."

I asked whether George lied before or if he was lying now. What this expert told me was that the model of lifelong confessing, over and over again, an AA model, doesn't work well for sex offenders. It's too stigmatizing, and they don't want to go through all that emotional agony with every new relationship of explaining why they did what they did and proving they understand how wrong it was. So, after the treatment, they make up a convenient lie to tell others. He added that the testing, at least one test he performed on George, indicated no attraction to young girls, not then, when George was first arrested, or now. In his view, what George did three years ago may have been a moral slip, committed during a stressful time when his thinking was impaired, his conscience on hold; that George's crime was what the expert called one "of opportunity" rather than one of preference.

Should George be allowed unsupervised visits with his daughter? The group therapist I also contacted, who noted that George had passed through group with shining colors, even becoming a role model for the other men, still said no. Why not? For him, once you've sexually abused a child, you have lost all rights to parent your own child. For me, I was not so sure, but I yielded to the man who knew George best because he thought the best of him despite his record. And if supervised visits were allowed to continue, George would see his daughter, consistently, continually, over the years to come, and the two of them, by the time she turned eighteen, will have a way of talking or not talking about that distant event. She will not lose a father. He will not lose a daughter.

Some lies that parents tell me work, and I have to live with the consequences of having believed them. Once a DCF worker warned me that something was off about a couple, that he couldn't put his finger on it. I ignored his concern, wondering if his sense of something wrong was due to the fact that this couple was gay. I should have known better. One of the more fantastic things about foster care in Vermont is the number of same-sex couples who adopt children, children of all ages, and give them loving homes. It's probably one of the major reasons I believe in the foster-care system. I have seen couples take tremendous, heart-wrenching chances. It is a risk, because to foster a child in hopes of adopting means you are opening yourself up to loss if the child is returned to the birth parents. You may also be opening yourself up to children with learning problems in school or developmental trauma to unwind. You will need to constantly be an advocate for this child. And when she or he is an adolescent, you may be opening yourself up to unimaginable anger and resentment. I could offer a dozen stories of gay couples parenting DCF children through adoption, some rather heroic, like the two men nurturing an eleven-year-old girl who was yet to be truly potty-trained. She was a big girl who would fly into rages, unfathomable rages over the denial of a second helping at dinner. While others might have seen a monster, these men saw a little girl and took her to Girl Scouts and swimming lessons. They read to her at night and taught her yoga and other mindfulness strategies to tame the beast within. When I met with her and asked her if she ever felt safe in the world, she said, "With my daddies and at Girl Scouts. I love my daddies."

In this case, though, I should have listened to the DCF worker warning me that something was off. One of the moms in this family, let's call her Beth, was so much more of a mother to the foster child than the other mom, Lexa, and had basically raised her as the primary attachment figure. That was what I'd observed in my office. But in the home observation, something felt wrong. How could Beth, such a loving mom, a mom who had once been a kindergarten teacher, live in a house with so few toys? The toys they did have weren't in reach but were delivered from on high, dropped down to the floor for playtime, from the other mother. I dismissed this as having to do with my own penchant for clutter, turning my preference into a liability and thinking that stricter parents maybe have more successful children. This child will grow up to make the most of his playtime.

Long after adoption, I learned that the couple had lied to me. When they were in my office, they knew that they were about to break up and had pretended to be a loving couple. Perhaps they believed that they could co-parent effectively as divorced parents, as so many divorced parents do. Perhaps they didn't want to muddy the already complicated issues of the case. But I don't like being lied to, and though I might not have returned the child to his birth mother, I may have had helpful recommendations for these two if they had spoken the truth. After they adopted this two-year-old boy, Eddy, they tried to co-parent, but the loss of her partner, for Beth, the nurturing mother, was too much, and she had a breakdown. Beth became so depressed she was hospitalized, and this gave Lexa a way of arguing that Beth shouldn't see the child at all, that Beth would be too unreliable, in and out of this child's life. It was time for little Eddy to have a chance to bond with her, Lexa. But he didn't, so I was told. And Eddy will grow up longing for two lost mothers, his biological mother and Beth. I only know this because of what another social worker told me. I often ask about former cases and people talk, although they probably aren't supposed to. But, somehow, being tricked and lied to makes us angry enough to gossip and seek comfort about our own parts in these messes.

———

During Family Weekend at Willy's rehab, there was one night when parents were permitted to take their children out of the center and have dinner out at one of the restaurants in town. This was to be the night where our sons would come clean to us. Willy, and all the young men, had practiced for this night, and he was brimming with honesty, in control and eager to tell me everything but not more than I wanted to know, urging me to ask him more questions, and proudly telling me the absolute truth, speaking small proud self-corrections, "no, that's not quite right, not honest enough" before he told a truer truth.

In the restaurant, Willy glowed. He was muscular and no longer heroin thin. He was clean-cut, like a private in the AA army, sturdy and forthright. He wanted me to know everything I wanted to know and to be happy for him and where he was now in his recovery. He was so confident that he had been saved, but I felt confused, withholding, and untrusting.

We ate the ceviche and then the fish tacos. After, we leaned on the rental car in the parking lot under bright crisscrossing spotlights from the streetlamps, and I asked him, "Was it a lie when you . . ."

"Yes."

"Were you telling the truth when you . . . ?"

"No."

"Do you remember when you . . . ?"

"Yes, that was a lie. I was going to buy drugs."

"Did you steal money from me?"

"Yes."

"Did you steal money from Dad?"

"Yes."

"Did you steal from Julian?"

"Yes."

"Why?"

"I was an addict. I am an addict."

"Why did you sell my guitar?"

"Because I needed money. When you're desperate, you're selfish. I was selfish. I was only thinking about getting drugs."

"Why didn't you sell the trombone?"

"I don't know. Maybe I would have."

"And the ukulele?"

"Yes, I sold it. I'm sorry."

"Where?"

"I don't know. Maybe Guitar Center?"

We passed the lies back and forth under the light in the parking lot, connecting each lie to the truth and then to addiction.

"That big argument in the kitchen?"

"No. I wasn't high then. I was just mad."

"What about your therapist?"

"I lied to him too."

"I should have known."

"No, you couldn't have."

"I should have seen you were lying."

"I was a good liar. I was a very good liar."

I would hold on to that statement for years to come. What a gift he gave me then and there. And yet it was his story, not mine. I should have known.

8. THE CAUSE OF ADDICTION

I've tried to imagine what taking heroin feels like. Every literary description leaves me wanting. A warm feeling that comes over you. Peace. The feeling of being freed from worries. Feeling like your truest self. Pure pleasure. Like the first bite of an excellent meal? The first sip of an expensive wine? The time in eighth grade when Steve Michaels held my hand for four blocks while walking me home? Sex? An orgasm? Lying on a blanket in the grass on a sunny day? A birthday party with all the people you love at it? In the groove with your chorus when it's singing in tune? Joyce DiDonato pulling a legato line gently through to its highest note? Holding your teenage son's feet on your lap while he watches TV? Holding your baby son to your breast? Oxytocin is released when a mother nurses her infant. Oxytocin. Oxycontin. A small rearrangement of letters marks the difference between the chemical of connection and the chemistry of separation.

Willy has told me that, after the first rush of pleasure, taking Oxycontin was just a way to feel all right. Oxycontin produces an initial feeling of euphoria, followed by feelings of relaxation and satisfaction. But I still want to know what is the cause of addiction.

Drug addiction seems different nowadays, no longer viewed as a moral problem or even an individual's choice. It's a brain disease. The director of NIH's National Institute on Alcohol Abuse and Alcoholism summarizes it: "The brain actually changes with addiction, and it takes a good deal of work to get it back to its normal state."

I love this explanation because it generally lets me off the hook. His brain was "hijacked." He let a terrorist onto the plane and his brain was hijacked. Many articles on the physiology of addiction show this in illustrations of MRI scans with their bright, pretty, glowing colors. There is more yellow there in that section, more purple here in this other section. The normal brain has more turquoise there, more green here. Proof arrives in phosphorescent, psychedelic colors, like an LSD awakening.

Even though scientists try to engage me, a nonscientist, with their colorful images, neuroscience bores me. Neuroscience teaches me that dopamine is a neurotransmitter, a chemical in the brain, the passage of which between neurons creates certain feelings. It asks me to understand the work of these things called neurons, with long skinny branches that end with large bits that send or receive stuff.

I can visualize the space in between a bunch of neurons now. Maybe it's like a ball pit in a McDonald's, where parents I see often have a supervised "community visit" with their kids. Some neurons are spewing colorful balls of dopamine into the ball pit, and some are vacuuming them up. Normally when people are experiencing pleasurable things, lots of colorful balls are released into the pit. Happy. Then, after a while, the balls get sucked up by neurons. If some of the balls don't get picked up by hovering hoovering neurons, then the ball pit is eventually emptied anyway by the balls getting sucked back into their original spots. I think. Does it matter?

I am not a scientist, and so I cling to any metaphor a scientist uses. Sometimes dopamine increases are represented by violet rocket ships, zooming the neurotransmitter from one part of the brain to the pleasure centers. Eating and sex launch violet rockets of dopamine to the pleasure centers, but maybe not at the same time.

Opiates are sneaky little pleasure imposters. They trick the brain. Opiates go to the dopamine receptors and latch onto them, taking the place of the real dopamine. Like the fake movie stars who take the seats of real movie stars at the Academy Awards when the real movie stars have to go to the bathroom. Like the grubby kid who pushed your butt out of a chair during musical chairs in kindergarten. They prevent those dopamine receptors from taking up or re-taking up the real dopamine. The ball pit is open all night. Violet rocket ships zoom and zoom. The addict stumbles down deliriously happy.

I'm not sure exactly why receptors for dopamine decrease during drug addiction, why eventually there are fewer of them. Maybe, as in musical chairs, one seat is pulled away with each turn. Are there fewer places for the rockets to zoom to? One study of monkeys on cocaine showed that after a year of cocaine abuse, they had a 21 percent reduction in D2 receptors. The D stands for dopamine. What results is depression. Anhedonia. Decreased sensitivity to pleasure, to the natural response to good things in life, even to the drug.

Neuroscience makes me feel less guilty as a mother, but more hopeless. Brain explanations are so deterministic. I feel better in the loving arms of behaviorists. Behaviorists see addiction as a learned behavior. For behaviorists, cravings are triggered by cues, some of which don't even have to be consciously received. You're going to the movie theatre and you start thinking of popcorn. You see a movie with drugs in it and you get a craving. You come home to visit your parents in Vermont, and every grocery store parking lot, every library, every park, Church Street itself is a trigger.

Behavioral psychologists don't use the word "unconscious," but they also don't use the word "choice," or only rarely. Behaviorists say, "Very powerful cravings, a hundred times greater than your craving for coffee in the morning." And that is why I am fond of them. Behaviorists agree with neuroscientists that addiction is a chronic illness, similar to diabetes, hypertension, asthma. Those afflicted with any of these will relapse at similar rates, in terms of following or not following their treatment regimens. Normal motivation for healthy behavior is gone, and normal braking systems don't work. Recovery is long term. But for behaviorists, changing the rewards can help.

Along with neurons and habits, another explanation offered for why addicts can't help being addicts has to do with trauma. Those who were traumatized by abuse in their childhood or the chaos of living in poverty, who were witnesses to murders, who were veterans of war, are susceptible. Yet the thinking about trauma is that here, too, the brain has been hijacked, and "the body keeps the score." The body remembers what the mind tries to avoid.

After a lifelong desire to see disorders as inventions of psychiatrists paid off by Big Pharma, I yield in soft complacency to the biological explanations. Like heroin, they make me relax and find peace. I don't have to look at myself, what I did or didn't do. I don't have to obsessively turn over in my mind the mistakes I made, the missed opportunities, the ways I fucked up. It's like Jesus offering relief or forgiveness. If I only yield to a loving savior, I can find peace. So why do I resist?

9. PARENTS WEEKEND

The first thing they tell the parents on Parents Weekend at Transitions is that your child may die from this disease. For some parents, this is a shock. For others, this is all we have been thinking about, from home, to the airport, to the hotel, to the morning in a windowless room facing two rehab therapists.

Next to me is a man I want to comfort. With a middle-aged build, sturdy and soft, he is awkwardly wearing leisure clothes when it seems he would be more comfortable in a suit. He earnestly takes notes on a small, lined notepad, asking the leaders questions as if the answers will tell him what to do next. He maintains an air of being in charge while he is totally helpless. His daughter sits beside him, dressed simply in jeans, a button-down shirt, and a sweater, like a graduate student, the smartest in the class, eager too, like her father, and clearly the good child in the family, taking care of both her father and her brother, Matthew, through this time. As with my family, there is an absence. For them, it's the mother; for me, my husband. Do the most frightened stay behind? Or did I say I wanted to go alone? Do I make Paul the rock who anchors us in Vermont? Or do I protect him from the world and keep him close to his piano because that's what's best for him? All I know is that I wanted to go alone.

Our night of truth under the lamppost light was to come in the middle of the visit. When we first arrived, none of us had seen our children clean and sober for a very long time. The last time we saw them, they were either high or in withdrawal. Some of the parents brought their children here against their will. Some bribed them. And others sent children who were ready to go. Some drove their kids to the address and walked them right on up to the turquoise front door. Others, like myself, put them on buses or planes, to be met by the representative we spoke to on the phone, a nice touch, a cord stretching from Vermont to Texas through the representative, Brian, the one who hooked me.

Then we see our kids, but briefly. Willy is no longer dangerously thin but strong and muscular—shining. We hug a long hard hug, sensing the strength in it and when to let go. When I look at him, I search for addiction, and he sends back to me rays of confidence.

"How's it going?"

"Good. Really good."

"This is a good place?" I ask him, looking for reassurance that we made the right choice.

"Yes."

The children take the parents on individual tours to see the dorm rooms, decorated in a Western style, the backyard, the meeting rooms, the cafeteria. The food, Willy tells me, is amazing, and when we walk through the kitchen, he takes two chocolate-chip cookies off a tray set out for all, handing one to me. He introduces me to the chef. As we walk through the hacienda, many young men stop and say, "Hi, Willy," and Willy introduces me to them. Like wherever Willy used to be, he was a guy's guy, the kind of boy other boys looked up to, the guy other guys wanted to show off for, a buddy, a bro. Willy's grandfather once speculated that it was Willy's aloofness that drew people to him. I thought instead it was his humor, which his grandfather didn't see or notice, a humor that was sometimes offensive or jarring but intimate nonetheless.

Later Willy and I meet with Willy's therapist, a large Mexican American woman who seems to know Willy, how he fooled us and how he fools himself. She talks about her own past addiction and encourages me to go to Al-Anon. I tell her that I am already going, which impresses her. Willy tells me afterward that she frequently cancels their appointments.

"What happens then?" I ask.

"It doesn't matter. There are all kinds of other people here that I talk to all day long. I like Luís the best."

There is a talk by the man who owns the Mercedes parked out front. He is also the owner of the rehab. And later there is another talk by the owner's son, who owns a Porsche, Willy tells me. Willy loves cars and notes who drives what, what model, what year. S class. 911.

On the second day of Parents Weekend, a talk that is supposed to be delivered by Willy's therapist is scheduled for eleven, but she hasn't shown up. I was looking forward to this talk because it was to be on parenting an addicted child. It seems that nobody knows why she isn't there, and the parents see the staff mumbling to each other not quite behind the scenes. It isn't the therapist's actual workday, but she knew that she was on the Parents' Weekend schedule. She didn't even call in to say she was sick apparently. This reminds me of Willy.

So, the staff pushes a reluctant well-dressed woman in Texas hair, high heels, and a white pantsuit to the front of the room. It turns out that she is the wife of the man who owns the rehab. She gives a talk instead of Willy's therapist, a talk about what it is like to be the partner of someone with an addiction.

She is like almost every speaker in AA or NA or Al-Anon and tells a story that goes, I was lost but now I'm found, was blind but now I see. Each speaker relishes the details of the downfall far too much. I suppose the harder they fell, the more glorious the rising, and the better the story. The former addicts are the worst. They ate pills by the dozens; they shot up several times a day until there were no veins left; they stole from their mothers, aunts, grandmothers, and even children ("Didn't I *even* raid my daughter's piggy bank"); they were arrested and found drugs in jail; they slept on the streets ("And if you ever slept on the street, lord have mercy, that ain't no feather bed"); they used dirty needles ("There but for the grace of God I did *not* get the AIDS"); they cheated on loved ones and loved ones left them; they lied, and lied, and lied, until there was nobody left to believe them. They describe all this with wonder and merriment. We at Al-Anon chuckle along, but I don't know why.

The wife of the owner describes her husband at his worst: "And there he was, under the coffee table, vomit next to him, the car outside crashed up on into the front of the garage, lookin' like an accordion, and I just picked up my keys, got my Gucci bag, and on the way out, said, 'Bye-bye, honey. Goin' grocery shoppin' for a spell.'" The audience laughs heartily at her decision to go on with life simply and without pain, detached, neutral to his agony, abandoning him there.

But we are the parents. Parents don't have the same options as wives. I'm irritated that they didn't have a speaker who is a parent and could speak of the difficulties of knowing when to help and when to walk away. The wife's point is that she isn't going to clean up after him anymore or help him to sober up. He will have to face his own consequences and sleep in his own vomit. A mother can't do that.

Later, a therapist runs a group in which we sit silently for the first fifteen minutes while putting pen to worksheet paper to complete sentence stems: "I was angry when you . . ." "What I want is for you . . ." "My worst fear is . . ." "The night you . . ." After we complete our lists, a tête-à-tête occurs in the middle of the circle, where each couple, addict and mother or addict and father, simply reads their statements to each other with no comments or discussion.

"Ha ha," Willy says to one kid in imitation of the playground bully on *The Simpsons*, the two-note sing-song every kid recognizes.

"You have to do two." This kid has to complete two sets of statements since he has both parents with him.

I find the other parents' statements more moving than Willy's and my statements to each other. I don't recall his. Willy also doesn't remember mine. Why would we remember any but our own failures?

I remember the Christian couple next to me, stiff and separated in the scooped seats of their plastic chairs, who talked about God and Jesus and used the word "blessed" in every other sentence. I don't think they were religious fanatics, but they spoke in a way that nobody back East would speak, with a presumption that everybody loved Jesus and we all, in the end, went to the same church. Willy told me that their son's older brother had died of a heroin overdose in an airport bathroom on his way to a rehab. Their second son is now an addict but doesn't want to be there, Willy has told me, and can't wait to get out of there to see his girlfriend, who is also an addict. I think about his suffering. He's stocky and masculine, and I'm betting does not allow himself to grieve for his brother. His parents must be so angry, so scared, so tried when they search for anything, a moment that they can still find "blessed."

The mom of the hairdresser who, Willy tells me, is gay and a cocaine addict pulls me over after this session. I stand with her outside the turquoise door while she has a cigarette.

"This is his fourth rehab," she confesses.

"Wow," I say, praying that this will be Willy's only rehab.

"This one's good. It's better than the others. They really know what they're talking about," she says, and I nod and smile in agreement.

"You know I remortgaged my home to pay for this," she confides. "I don't want him to know, though. Please don't mention this to Willy."

I promise her I won't tell Willy she has remortgaged her home. Later I tell her secret to Willy, though, to let him know, through her story, the kinds of sacrifices mothers make. And Willy lets me know that her son is not serious about his recovery, which makes me enormously sad.

There is also a lovely, poised woman who remains removed and seemingly doubtful, present but never really joining the others in the hopeful moments that the weekend is supposed to evoke, however falsely conjured. I so desperately want her to join the crowd, to be hopeful. She tells me, though, that this is the fifth rehab for her husband, an alcoholic. He may not have a job when he gets out of re-hab. He was drunk at his daughter's college graduation. She "can't do this anymore." We all have our stories, stories we want to hang over our addicts' heads in dark storm clouds. And even if, during Parents Weekend, we're still feeling lost, angry, and heartbroken, this is not the place to dwell on those responses.

I observe an odd family grouping of a mother and father, close, hostile, enmeshed, with a tag-along younger beauty. Is this the mother's sister? An older daughter from a former marriage? She is wearing a flowery ankle-length dress and dangling earrings, looking like a hippie chick from LA. It turns out she is a hippie chick from LA and the father's new wife who most likely insisted, "I'm a part of this family too." I am concerned for the boy's mother and what she may be feeling on this difficult weekend. But I know from my therapy practice that stepmothers can do a lot for a child who rejects both his parents, yet who still needs parenting. She is another mother of sorts, and the first mother in desperation will need to tolerate her and maybe eventually even thank her if this weekend succeeds.

A brassy, busty, big-haired blond lady enters our circle of plastic chairs like a cowboy walking into a saloon. She is here for "Family Time" and gives one of the weekend's better pep talks, with Texan witticisms and AA slogans popping at us faster than double-striked lightning, than a sneeze through a screen door, than a scalded ape, than—and so on. We are told we are lucky to get her for this day given that she moves from rehab center to rehab center across Texas doing her talks, a much sought-after speaker, one who could talk the legs off a chair. She passes out a worksheet with some old-school charm and information on it.

"Here are the four types of people in the alcoholic family. Which one are you?" There are cartoon outlines of each type that look like they were drawn in the 1960s. Mothers wear aprons. Fathers wear hats and ties. The sons are on scooters. The daughters have ribbons in their hair.

We perform role-plays of these characters. Who am I? I wonder. Who is the clown, who distracts the family? Who is the scapegoat? Who is the hero? Who is the rescuer? Who is the enabler?

When I'm in charge, in the classroom, I like role-plays, although they make my students anxious. It's so hard to be empathic and reflective on the spot, in front of an audience. At Transitions, in these rehab role-plays, the addict is to play him or herself, and the parent is to act out with him a typical interaction involving one of these stereotyped characters. I can just feel that this woman is itching to have someone break down and cry for the purpose of making these role-plays meaningful. (Former addicts still love drama.) If someone cries, and hardened family members soften and embrace, she can go home satisfied, full as a tick.

The role-plays progress, some intense and some jolly. Then Matthew is encouraged to get in the center of the circle and speak to his absent mother. Matthew is the boy that the golfer father and studious sister are worried about, and so they are all for this. The boys in the room encourage him too. They know something the rest of us don't know about Matthew and his mother, something he may have revealed in group therapy or in a late-night discussion in the backyard, where the guys go to smoke. Someone is asked to play Matthew's mother to give him a figure to speak to. Matthew resists, but with enough pressure from his friends, he self-consciously gets up and stands in the middle of the circle, his father and sister straining forward with hope and concern. The guys around the circle shout encouragements. He is young, tall, awkward, and stuck in the middle like an ape in a round cage. The blond lady is gentle and cajoling, saying, "It's all right, sweetheart," but you can see he feels as if he is being poked with a stick. He just stands there turning red, his arms hanging but his fists clenched. Is he going to cry? He is younger than a lot of the other guys. He doesn't want to cry in front of them, or us, or his father and his sister.

Willy offers to do the role-play with him, next to him, doubling his feelings and thoughts, as this is something the boys have learned to do in role-plays. We all think that Matthew will talk now, with Willy by his side. He opens his mouth. He closes it. Willy ventures a guess at what Matthew might say if he were to talk. Matthew then holds his ground and says nothing, staring at the floor. The role-play ends with a disappointment. Matthew has not had the breakthrough he needs. Willy comes back to sit next to me and whispers, "That is one angry dude."

When we are saying goodbye to our children, the day after the role-plays, Matthew's sister takes me aside. Her father joins her. They both ask me if I will ask Willy to look after Matthew. Willy has been seen by these other parents as a leader, a role model, and a shining example of what rehab can do. They make me feel as if I made the right choice, that rehab is working. In fact, the blond lady approached me quietly at the end of the day, putting her arm around my shoulders, saying, "Mama, you oughta thank yourself for raising such a fine boy. Willy is pert near my very favorite ever. Mama, if he don't make it, I swear on God's green earth, nobody can!" Willy had been a mensch at rehab, an active participant, someone who found hope there and gave himself over to the twelve-step homework, figuring out what kind of higher power he could relate to, even though he wasn't given a god growing up. The kids at rehab looked up to him, and the older guys saw him as a pal. I felt proud. I felt lucky. Willy was going to be all right. I said I would talk to Willy about Matthew, and I knew Willy would help.

Matthew left rehab early though, just a few days after Parents Weekend, against the advice of the staff. Willy told me this in a phone call. At eighteen, Matthew was an adult and couldn't be kept there against his will. Two weeks later, he was dead.

10. SUBOXONE

I wake up at five in the morning. He is unsafe. I know it. I've been blind again. It was an email from a former student, Elise, that woke me up. I read it before bed, which is a sure sign I won't sleep through the night. I have the luck of being able to fall asleep within three, no two, minutes of putting my head to pillow. Staying asleep is a different matter.

Elise had been a good student and became a good counselor during the year in which she worked at the Robideau Center in Burlington in homes for traumatized children. She revealed to me privately back then that she was in recovery, a former heroin addict who started as an Oxy addict. A former competitive distance runner in high school, she started taking opiates that had been prescribed to her after an injury and follow-up surgery. When the prescriptions ran out, the Oxies, at around eighty dollars a pill, were too expensive, and so she substituted with heroin.

In the email I'd received earlier in the evening, Elise confessed to me, years after she had graduated, that she had relapsed after graduation. When she was my student, she had been on Suboxone for over three years, and when she relapsed, she wrote, she was still on Suboxone, though only a small dose by that time. "Suboxone saved my life," she once told me, and she stayed on it, a small dose, for security.

Doctors have differed over the years in their opinions on how long an addict needs to stay on Suboxone. A year, two years, seven years, as long as they want to? Elise kept taking a small dose because she was afraid of a relapse.

Suboxone is a combination of buprenorphine and naloxone: four parts bupe to one part naloxone. Buprenorphine is the opiate. Naloxone is the opiate blocker used in emergency rooms to resuscitate people who overdose. Buprenorphine sits in the seats in the brain that have been reserved for heroin, so the emptiness of those seats doesn't create withdrawal symptoms or cravings to be filled. They call it a *partial* agonist because it doesn't fit well in those seats. If it did, it would get someone high in the same way that opiates do. But it crams in well enough to stop the cravings and mood swings. Unlike opiates, which you need to take more and more of in order to feel good, Suboxone has a ceiling effect, and you don't have to increase the dose to feel all right. Those on Suboxone don't take it to feel good but to feel normal.

Suboxone, however, is "sticky" in the brain, Elise wrote, making it hard to get it out of the system. Nobody really knows the drug's long-term effects either; they just know that if you take people off Suboxone, they have trouble staying clean. Elise wrote that now doctors see that it replaces the natural production of endorphins, just as heroin does over time. And while she felt great at the beginning of Suboxone treatment, after years on the drug, it made her feel sluggish and tired all the time.

Stay on a short time. Stay on a long time. Stay on forever if it works. Doctors disagree. But the folks at some NA meetings treat you like you're still on drugs if you take it. They know too many addicts who abuse bupes.

Once opiates dried up in Vermont, the mothers I evaluated were taking bupes sold on the street. I didn't understand why they would buy a street version rather than go to a doctor to prescribe the Suboxone, virtually giving them the drug for free. But I learned from one mother that if they slip up and abuse them or if they are caught selling them—if they do anything that shows they are not dead serious about recovery—they're kicked out of the doctor's practice or put back at the end of the waiting list for treatment so that someone more reliable is moved up. There is so much punishment of addicts, but when Suboxone is in short supply and there aren't enough doctors who can prescribe it, I understand the doctors' cold perspective. Most doctors aren't therapists; they are prescribers. They don't have time to mess around with the ambivalence of the addicts towards a drug that gives them a taste of a high but prevents a high. And they have heard too many stories, too many lies. It's better to have a policy to follow than to have to listen to the stories and guess at the truth.

After FDA concerns delayed its release, the first form of Suboxone, an individually wrapped film with a traceable bar code, was approved in 2010. The film strip Willy uses is patent protected until 2023, and he carries it home in a lockbox. The makers of Suboxone have done what many pharmaceutical companies have done: change the drug enough after its patent has expired in order to keep it expensive. There has been a campaign of "fear-based messaging" against a newer tablet form, the cheaper form of Suboxone, in order to per-suade addicts to take the more expensive film.

Vivitrol might be a better solution for the mothers I evaluate. Un-fortunately, Vivitrol is an injection that insurance companies do not support. Of course they don't support it. It costs $1,100 a shot, one shot a month. It forces addicts to cope as best they can and find new forms of coping because drugs won't have an effect after the injection. I've wondered now and then whether we should offer to pay for this. It's expensive, but other mothers have remortgaged their houses. Do not offer what he hasn't asked for, recommends a parenting coach.

Elise is clean now after going to Mexico to get ibogaine treat-ment. Ibogaine is touted as a miracle cure and is used in West Africa in religious ceremonies to produce hallucinations. It's also featured in the TV show *Homeland*, in which Damian Lewis plays a veteran and a US senator and possibly a spy needing to beat his addiction fast. After an ibogaine treatment, there are no withdrawal symp-toms, and some say it feels as if a reset switch has been flicked on for your life. But the patient goes through hell and back to get there. As in *The Magic Flute*, where there are three trials—fire, water, and silence—the addict will go through three days of hallucinations and incredible agitation. Although I have learned to hate the insurance companies with all my being, and to understand the deep corruption and conflicts of interest among Big Pharma and the FDA, there is still something very American in me that feels that if the FDA in the US hasn't approved a drug, it must be too dangerous to take.

In some states, like Texas, Suboxone costs $500 a month. In oth-ers, like Vermont and Massachusetts, it can be free. It should be free. Johann Hari, who wrote *Chasing the Scream*, reported on successful programs in Portugal and Vancouver that decriminalize addiction and give addicts what they need when they need it.

The alarm clock is ticking, like a robotic cricket. The peepers are peeping their raucous song in the pond outside. I don't feel Willy is safe, and so I toss in bed and poke my feet out of the covers to cool them. Paul gets up and goes to sleep in the guestroom after a terse exchange.

"What's wrong?"

"Nothing . . . Willy."

"What? What happened?" He is in panic mode instantly.

"Nothing new, nothing different. Just worried."

"Ach."

Tonight will not be one of those nights where we lie awake together.

I don't know what to do in the middle of the night. Willy may relapse. Maybe not this year but maybe, like Elise, in ten years. He may die. I texted Willy at eleven, before I fell asleep.

R u ok? How r u?

I fell asleep before an answer. I know better than to wait for an answer. He is not in this world to calm my worries. My worries are a burden to him. I wait out the night in the darkness, with the crickets marking time, the peepers chorusing below.

11. A FATHER IN RECOVERY

Jay is no longer an addict, but how did that happen without Suboxone? Why do some addicts succeed without it and others don't? He seems to be doing everything right to get his son back. He is working on a landscaping crew and attending therapy. He has a girlfriend who's a yoga instructor. He goes to AA meetings and has plans for starting his own landscaping business. When he plays with his son, he is both playmate and father. He follows the six-year-old around on hands and knees and toots the train horn as his son makes the train approach a crossing. He vrooms for the race cars and fixes the tracks when they become detached. But he also sets limits when limits are needed. "Yes, we can play with that Nerf bow and arrow, but we don't point it at people. No. No. Would you like a time-out? Thank you."

This child is comfortable here in Vermont, even though his mother is gone. Her rights have been terminated, and she is not permitted to see her son. She may be in California. She may be around the corner, and as many children in foster care do, he may run into her some time. There are three sets of grandparents, two sets of aunts and uncles, and a pair of former foster parents who want to care for him, all stable loving people with faults that keep them fighting among themselves. But his father, Jay, has rights even if he has been away. If his abandonment is framed not as abandonment but as his need to get away from Vermont because of the drugs, maybe he has a chance.

The DCF social worker is suspicious of Jay and wants me to hear her out, so we set up a separate phone call to discuss the case. Isn't Jay to blame for the child's mother's addiction? She was so young when she met him and he introduced her to the hard stuff. Have I not read the police report of his violence? There was a restraining order against him. Did he not smash three cars while driving high? DCF workers trust in recovery when they work with mothers who have addictions, but they tend not to trust that violent men can ever become gentle.

I enjoyed meeting with this dark-haired burly man with big hands he kept still on knees that moved up and down. He told me he regularly attends cigar enthusiast conventions and trade shows. His own father, before descending into alcoholism and drug abuse, owned an online cigar business, which he gave to his son to carry on. Jay is trying to revive this business in Georgia as a sideline to the landscaping business.

I wonder in my interview why Jay can't come back to live in Vermont, where his little boy has so many family members who love him and who have cared for him. I believe, perhaps wrongly, that the schools and health care will be better here than in Georgia. Jay's answer is a good one for a former addict: Vermont is a trigger. Every street corner, dirt road, old friend, even every crazy snowstorm carries with it a memory of using, leading to a craving, leading to using. Perhaps more importantly, though, he has a girlfriend who has a daughter in Georgia, and she shares custody with her ex and so cannot move out of state. This girlfriend has never used drugs. She is stable and getting her master's degree in social work.

The police report in front of me, with words that frighten, like "blood," "bruises," "unconscious," "severe," makes me understand the DCF social worker's fears. As with the pattern of lying that becomes second nature to the addict when using, I wonder if the social work-er's fears have become a pattern. There isn't a pattern of violence though. Jay doesn't even remember that one horrible night, the night that lost him his visits with his son, but he remembers his girlfriend in the hospital the next day, forgiving him. His best friend had died the week before in a snowmobiling accident, and Jay had been high out of his mind all week, as had his girlfriend. She was sorry because she had been taunting him that night about some other guy she had had sex with. That's in the paperwork in front of me too. She took the blame for his violence, even as she was waking up from her coma in her hospital bed.

I don't let Jay off the hook, but I don't think he is lying when he says he doesn't remember that night. Once someone has com-mitted that kind of violence, should they ever be able to care for a child? That's the question I have to answer. I ask myself, Why the hell do we send these guys to batterers' intervention groups if we don't believe they can change? I recall that it takes over a year in one of those groups for most men to even admit to the violence. Yet I see Jay love his little boy and imagine him teaching his son about cigars, although he himself rarely smokes these days, taking the AA perspective that one addiction supports another.

If I don't recommend that Jay be given a chance to parent his son, am I protecting his son from potential danger or am I punishing Jay for what he did? What would I say to the judge to support the point of view that Jay can't parent his own child, that once violent, there is always the potential for violence? Then the judge would ask me for evidence of this, and I would have to say there is little evidence to support this view. I could cite the research that domestic violence typically also carries with it physical violence towards the children, that knowing your father beat your mother is a sort of psychological violence inflicted on the child. But Jay's son didn't see this happen, and the single incident was almost five years ago.

I watch them. His little boy is tentative but not because he fears his father. He doesn't know him well enough to judge whether the stories he has overheard are true. Maybe he deserves a chance to be parented by a father who is clean and cares for him. It is possible to prevent his losing all the other family members—grandparents, aunts, uncles, cousins—if I recommend that he spends his summers in idyllic Vermont. If I recommend a trial period in Georgia with a return in the summer to Vermont, that might work. Yes. Jay will start with a visit over Christmas vacation, then during the spring, then a month in the summer, leaving more time for father to create stability in job and home, to find a therapist in Georgia for his son, for DCF to create a connection with social services down there, and for his little boy to get accustomed to the idea of change. In September, it will switch. The child will go to school in Georgia with his father caring for him. Vermont will be the place for visits and long summers, cooler summers than those in Georgia. His little boy will be welcomed with open arms by his Vermont family. This will work. What the court calls "reunification" becomes redemption. As long as Jay is not the violent man in the DCF reports. As long as Jay stays clean. After working with addicted parents for years, we all have our doubts.

12. IDYLLIC VERMONT

In spite of news stories naming Vermont one of the states with a serious opiate problem, most people who come to Vermont as tourists see it as an idyllic vacation spot. They come in leaf season to pick apples and drive down country roads, in the winter to go skiing, or in the summer for a lake vacation. There are plays to see, good music to hear, and excellent restaurants. There are smart liberals here, former hippies, who fight to preserve historic buildings and support community theatre. And as the world knows now, there is Bernie.

But there's another Vermont, the Vermont of empty roads that lead to nothing, to danger, or to death. The roads in Vermont that go on and on. If I let my mind wander when I drive and then refocus, I sometimes don't know if I'm on Spear Street or Dorset. Do I turn right at Cheese Factory Lane or go straight? Put on my brights during a snowstorm and the mesmerizing rays of snow attack my windshield. I risk sliding into oblivion. You can drop me in the middle of the poorest of city neighborhoods and I will feel more comfortable than if you were to leave me in the middle of nowhere in Vermont.

When we moved to Vermont in 1996 I felt as if I was banished to nowhere. The red Budweiser sign in the window of the small store at the end of our new block, the boats in driveways, the kids without helmets on bikes—all signaled something unsafe. I didn't see country roads, pretty barns, and covered bridges. I saw isolation, poverty, and harm. Trailers were everywhere and in the very same towns where McMansions were being constructed overnight in faux grandeur. While these mansions drew my scorn, the trailers made me afraid. So many isolated trailers in Vermont, set out in a field alone or behind a farmhouse. Next to them were broken-down cars and trucks.

Those trailers don't scare me anymore, although I have heard plenty of stories of harm done in trailers. I have also heard plenty of stories of harm done in single-family homes. Living as I do, on twelve acres up a lonely hill, I'm now even a bit envious of trailer-park neighborhoods where the children freely ride their Big Wheels up neighbors' walkways and run up and down the interconnecting smaller roads. Here is the community my children never had.

Homes are important, but people in Vermont also have the woods. The Vermont men I evaluate have the woods in a different way than do the people of my acquired socioeconomic class. These men hunt, hike, camp, track, and fish. They snowmobile, take out the ATV, "go jeeping" or "go tenting." They have things to teach their children in the woods. I have never heard a single bad memory from a child relating to the woods. Good father memories are formed in the woods in Vermont.

The wealthier middle class in Vermont also have their woods. They hike Camel's Hump and Mount Mansfield, go for meditative walks with their dogs, and write petitions against development of the land. These flatlanders don't often mix with the real Vermonters nor understand what their lives are like. They chat in their front yards with the man who comes to cut dead branches from their trees or re-dig their well. One might think the two would run into each other in the woods, one in a fluorescent orange vest walking a dog, the other hunting a deer, but that rarely happens. I know that for me, as soon as I hear a pop in the woods, I take my dog and skedaddle.

And maybe for socioeconomic or historical reasons (or both), there are virtually no people of color in Vermont, very few African Americans in particular. In my decades of work here, I have only worked on cases involving a handful of black women, no men.

Like a Rorschach blot, Vermont can be a paradise of sorts, with brown, orange, and red leaves whirling in the wind, or it can be something threatening, dark, formless, if you know it as part of the New England opiate epidemic. When Willy came home, from relapses, from rehabs, what Vermont did he see? Addiction doesn't cloud the brain; it focuses it. And if he was trying to stay clean, he most likely didn't see dancing leaves or the pleasant little candles in the frosty windows of warm houses or our pretty snowfalls. He saw those roads. Every long road he drove down in painful withdrawal desperate to find a pill. Every intersection at which he met a dealer. The addictions experts say that these places ping his brain, each matched to a craving. I understand why he needed to stay away.

13. MOTHER AND CHILD IN A CHURCH BASEMENT

Lori is on Suboxone, and her story is potentially a Suboxone success story. Potentially, because although she is clean, who knows if she will stay clean. Suboxone helps, but it doesn't guarantee success, and Lori had been clean and then relapsed before. When Lori had been clean for a year, on her one-year anniversary, after she had received her one-year coin at NA, an old boyfriend came to town on a motorcycle and took her out to the Champlain Valley Fair. Leaving her three-year-old daughter with friends, she relapsed for one wild weekend. On the Wednesday after her celebratory weekend, she called her old rehab and asked to be readmitted. Home is the place where, when you have to go there, they have to take you in, wrote Robert Frost, perhaps from his stone house in Southern Vermont. They took her in. Her daughter, Maribel, would have to stay at Lori's friends'

place a little longer, a friend who seemed to be managing her own sobriety and three children well. Driving to the rehab, Lori called her
DCF social worker to let her know what had happened. She would
later try to persuade me, "That counts for something, doesn't it? I
was honest, right away. I got help immediately. I took care of things."
That does count for something.

Lori left Maple Depot before the end of the first day because the
person who could prescribe Suboxone wasn't there that week. I don't
know whether she was merely chasing a high, however small, but
from what I have learned about the pain of withdrawal, she probably
wanted to avoid it at all costs. For some addicts, the next fix isn't
so much a desire to fly but a way to maintain their new normal and
avoid the godawful symptoms of fever, nausea, pains, and cravings.
She drove to a second Vermont rehab center, one she had lived at
before, called Plenty Good Room, and after getting her Suboxone,
she stayed there for ten days.

Lori told me during our interview that she enjoyed attending the
groups but had left this rehab early, against her therapist's advice,
because the place was "chaotic" and "they were constantly canceling
groups" she wanted to attend. I believed her, remembering how hard
it was even for a fancy rehab in Texas to provide consistent care. I
empathized with Lori's frustration, which ended in an impulsive decision she stuck with. I also understood that some people cope with
disappointment by rejecting the one who has disappointed them,
thinking, Who needs you?!

To Lori's credit, she stayed clean for about a month after she left
rehab, but she relapsed again when she heard what her daughter, now
in foster care, had reported to her foster mother. Maribel, having been
moved by DCF out of Lori's friends' home to a foster home that was
DCF approved with trained foster parents, had come to this home a
frightened and disoriented child. But in the new foster home, it was
as if she had been wandering in the woods and was now dazzled by
the light in a clearing that showed a lovely hut, with a thatched roof
and smoke rising from the chimney in a neat diagonal stream. It is
like that for many children placed in foster homes. After the initial

shock of separation and amid the deep emotions of loss, many foster children marvel at TV rooms, stocked pantries, and, especially, the basic organization of middle-class homes and family farms.

After settling in, Maribel began demanding to have all the windows and doors triple-checked at night before she went to sleep so that no "bad men" could come in. Even after the triple- and sometimes quadruple-checks, her foster parents would find Maribel in the morning sleeping under her bed rather than in it. A DCF investigation about these "bad men" led to a substantiation of sexual abuse by one of Lori's previous boyfriends.

I had seen Maribel a week earlier for the play interview, and after playing for half the session, we moved to the "grown up" side of my office. I turned on the tape recorder and, using the National Institute for Child Health and Development Investigative Interview Protocol for Young Victims and Witnesses, I asked the six-year-old the standard questions to elicit a narrative about the abuse and to uncover any additional abuse, starting with, "Tell me what happened." Then I went on to ask the suggested introductory questions about lying and truth telling, including having her practice saying "I don't know" if she didn't know an answer to a question, before moving on to other questions that are aimed at inviting a child to speak about the abuse. These questions are still quite general and do not lead the child.

She ended up first describing seeing her mother's boyfriend give her mother a black eye. After getting as many details as possible about this event, I asked another general question that led to her description of a night when her mother's boyfriend was babysitting.

"He, he, brought me to his bedroom."

"Okay. What happened in that room?"

"He was doing something impossible."

"He was doing something impossible. Can you tell me more?"

"I think that's all I can remember."

"You think that's all you remember right now. Is there anything else you might be able to remember?"

"He did sex to me like he did to my mother."

"What does that mean, he did sex?"

"He didn't know I was my mother's daughter because, because of the shoes that I was wearing."

That was all I got. That's the way young children reveal sexual abuse to you, in a way that the court will find unacceptable but that makes your insides go haywire while you struggle to maintain a calm demeanor. DCF had already substantiated the abuse, and I didn't want to push Maribel further.

Hearing about the abuse was the wind that sent Lori leeward into selling and using, then selling in order to use, and using to avoid withdrawal. So, DCF filed a termination of parental rights (TPR) order, which prompted Lori to tack back in the other direction, windward, and work at getting clean again. She began to use "smartly," so she said, only when she anticipated the need to ward off withdrawal and only until she could get on board at a place in Burlington that prescribed Suboxone, a place she would have to drive forty-five minutes each day to. Why so far? Because Lori had relapsed before, she was at the bottom of the waiting list for the site closer to her.

I don't envy the doctors who have to decide whether this person wants to get high or that person wants to get clean. But I fault a system in which the waitlist for legal Suboxone sends addicts, used to obtaining illegal drugs anyway, searching for illegal ways to get clean.

When Lori appeared in court to protest the TPR, she had been on Suboxone for only six months, but Maribel had been in foster care for a year and a half. Lori had a steady job and an NA sponsor who spoke on her behalf in court. The judge asked that DCF give her a little more time. So I was called in, to evaluate Lori, Maribel, and the two of them together in my office and at a visit in a church basement.

Maribel was another one of those little white waifs, a blond, underfed girl with haunted eyes and an unpleasant way of bossing around grownups just to be the boss, in a way that never brings relief. She sat on the dirty rug concentrating on building a Lego house for an imaginary cat named Dancy to live in "all by herself." Every time Lori tried to demonstrate to me and the Family Time coach some new parenting skill she had picked up in her parenting class, whether it was reflecting on what Maribel was doing, praising her daughter's work, or offering her a Lego piece to join the play, Maribel tightened her bony back, which was all her mother could see, and said, "No, I'm playing by myself."

"That's all right, honey," Lori said in a smooth voice. Patient.

"Don't call me 'honey.' I'm not your boyfriend."

Lori ignored this. "What are you makin' there?"

"I'm not telling."

"Can I help you with that piece?"

"No, I'll do it."

"I'm sorry, honey. I love you."

"I told you not to call me 'honey.'"

What Maribel was working on became increasingly frustrating to her. She couldn't get it right, but her face was as unmoving as a Lego figure, and she refused her mother's help. Finally, Maribel crawled over to the Family Time coach and meowed at her. The Family Time coach patted her and said, "Nice kitty," at which Maribel stood up, gave the coach the stubborn Lego pieces, and said, "Fix this." The Family Time coach fixed it and Maribel smiled and sat back down.

Lori was not fazed by this rejection and maintained a positive demeanor while she watched her daughter play and interact with the Family Time coach. Later she told me that her positive outlook came from the NA group she attends, which calls themselves Dopeless Hopefiends as opposed to Hopeless Dopefiends. She mentioned that her therapist, too, is always positive: "He deals in the moment, and not in the past."

The therapists of the parents sometimes speak to me willingly on their behalf. Child therapists are the most withholding. It is a strange dilemma for therapists that when they are treating children, the children really have no rights to privacy. Their parents or guardians have those rights, which include complete access to files on their children. Yet many psychotherapists believe they have a greater obligation to the child and do keep the play and the conversations they have with children private. They sense, and I sometimes agree, that revealing any part of the session can get in the way of successful treatment. For therapy to be a truly neutral safe haven, a place of ritual and surprise, a therapist has to protect the magic circle.

Maribel's therapist didn't return my calls, but Lori's therapist spoke to me. I asked him, "Is she ready to take a closer look at her responsibility for all this?" valuing insight as I tend to do. He said, "It's a journey, but it's not something we're focused on." This was one of the kinder ways of showing support for a client who may not be quite ready yet for the responsibilities of parenting. It's a journey, but it sounded as if she wasn't ready to look back.

Lori's daughter may not want to sail on this journey with her mother, snuggled in tight as she is within a home that is on solid ground. There she has two parents who triple-lock the doors and windows for her every night. I wonder to myself as I watch her play: Maybe Maribel doesn't need her mother. But that can't be so, no matter how much some children have wished this. Maybe the only way to relate to this new clean and sober mother is not to believe in her. I certainly can understand that. None of us want to be hopeful dopes.

The week before the observation visit, I asked Lori how her substance abuse had affected her daughter's life, and she said she used to be sick from withdrawal and not play with her. But she also claimed that most of the time that she was on drugs, she was using only to maintain, and that it didn't really interfere with her parenting. Looking down at the printouts of reports on my lap, I told her that DCF was concerned about her choice of boyfriends and their, um, influence on Maribel. She said that her choice of men was connected to her drug use and she would do better now.

That day, when I drove home and talked to the social worker on Bluetooth, which made the trip down the same old Vermont roads more tolerable, I was brought into her reality. Sure, Lori is passing all the urine tests, she said, but it may be that she is still selling. Neighbors have reported seeing drug dealers at her door. Lori denies it, but the social worker said she has heard that Lori has a new boyfriend who deals. When Maribel's school tried to include Lori in a parent-child event, she didn't show. That last bit of information is a clincher. She is still disappointing her daughter, and her daughter is rejecting her back.

Perhaps even more than Maribel, I want to believe in Lori's sobriety, her claim of a positive outlook, her therapist's trust in her journey. I don't want to look back either. But I haven't seen her parent Maribel. I have only seen Maribel reject her parenting.

At the end of the church visit, when the Family Time coach stated, "Ten minutes left," Maribel grabbed the snack her mother had brought her, a snack she had rejected earlier in the visit, and clutched it under a table in the corner of the room, like a seagull having snatched the last corner of a sandwich off a towel at the beach. She pulled a doll's quilt over her head saying she wanted to hide from her foster father. "Don't tell him where I am," she shouted from her little hidey-hole. She bossed her mother, saying, "If he asks where I am, say you love me and that I ran away."

The Family Time coach asked, "What would happen then?" and Maribel answered her, "Then he would leave without me. That would be cool."

"No, it wouldn't," the Family Time coach said back.

But Maribel stood her ground and said, "Yes it would, because then I could stay with my mama!" She hadn't finished rejecting Lori.

Maribel's foster father did come to pick her up, right on time, and Maribel couldn't stay hidden for more than two seconds before she jumped out and bounded into his arms. Being found, being seen, being safe—all triple-locked her heart. Her head on his shoulder, they left the DCF office. She was safe but tired. It is exhausting loving an addict.

PART III

Attachment

1. ATTACHMENT

Many of the evaluations I perform are what DCF calls "attachment evaluations." The agency suspects, as do I, that when attachment is strong between a parent and a child, it can withstand the ravages of addiction. Social workers want to know whether a child has a strong or weak attachment to the mother whom they haven't spent the last year with, the mother who neglected the child, or abandoned her, or harmed her in any other way, and whether freeing the child for adoption would cause trauma. They hope for a yes or no decision: the child is attached/the child is not attached.

Sometimes it is obvious what DCF is after and clear that they just want documentation from an expert. A child who was removed from his mother at birth, who has lived in the same foster home for two years, who has visited his mother for two hours a week at first and more recently twice a week—how could he be attached to her? Why would she be the person he chose to run to when fearful? His safe haven? He might like this affectionate woman and enjoy his visits with her. He could enjoy cuddling with her on the ratty DCF couch while she reads him a book. He could hug her hello and goodbye, just like a child would do if visiting a grandparent. He could even call her "Mommy." But attached? Most likely not.

Attachment is a controversial topic, the field developing as it did in the middle of the rise of second-wave feminism. John Bowlby, a psychoanalyst, built his theory of attachment with support from research studies in the 1940s and '50s, one showing that infants in orphanages did not thrive if they were only cared for physically; they also had to be held and nurtured. Another study, Harry Harlow's on rhesus monkeys, showed that the baby monkeys, when cruelly separated from their mothers, scampered to wire "mother" monkeys that provided food and water but returned to cling steadfastly to the terry-cloth versions when in need of comfort or when they were afraid. The babies did so even though the cloth "monkeys" provided no sustenance or response.

Bowlby saw attachment as a universal "motivational system" comparable to the Freudian drives of sex and aggression, and this thought was revolutionary at the time. What actually *was* revolutionary was Bowlby's idea that we are more or less "driven" to form attachments and are equipped with instinctive behaviors to facilitate this. Bowlby wrote that attachment is a human given; if infants anywhere are consistently attended to and responded to kindly and effectively, they will develop an emotional bond called attachment. Our survival depends on this. In moments of fear or uncertainty, the child seeks proximity, what Bowlby called "a safe haven."

We think of mothers as primary attachment figures, but anthropologists have shown that children around the world are raised by multiple attachment figures and that, even in cultures in which mothers tend to be the primary caregivers, there is variation with regard to how close to the mother a child is kept and what a mother needs to do to be good enough. We in the West favor independence and teach our babies to survive the separation of sleeping alone in the evening, encouraging them to explore the world much earlier than other mothers across the globe who spend their days with their babies, and later even their toddlers, wrapped tightly against their bodies.

This has been the problem with assessing attachment through the "Strange Situation," which is a very strange situation indeed for some toddlers. The Strange Situation is a research protocol that measures attachment. To understand what kind of attachment exists between a mother and a toddler, they are asked to play together in a research laboratory room, until the mother says goodbye and leaves the room, cued by the researcher. The mother returns for a while only to once again get up and leave the room without warning. A stranger enters and in a little bit the mother comes back. The child's reaction to the mother upon each return is key. Does he run to her, cling to her for dear life? Is he inconsolable, thinking: "How could you leave me?" Does he glance over, briefly nod, and then continue with his play? Does he act odd, confused, wandering around the room, first beating at her then grabbing on to her, adhering like Velcro?

The problem with making an assessment based on the Strange Situation is that if you are a Japanese baby and for the first year of your life have never been far from the body of your mother, this situation is incredibly strange. And if you are a baby who says goodbye to Mommy every morning when you go to daycare, then this situation is not so very strange. Culture and context is enormously important.

There are three kinds of insecure attachments: ambivalent/anxious, avoidant, and disorganized. The ambivalent/anxious child is distressed at separation and can't be soothed. This child *hyperactivates* the attachment system when threatened, becoming demanding and inconsolable. It is the only way to get attention from a less available mother. The avoidantly attached child is self-sufficient to her own detriment. She *deactivates* the attachment system when threatened. Why look for proximity if it can't be found? Better to rely on oneself. The third type, the disorganized attached child, is confused about whether to approach or withdraw, and so does both simultaneously, throwing all she's got at the attachment figure. Unsure and even frightened of what might be the response, she retreats, then advances, then retreats again. I saw a child at a visit run with open arms to his mother to embrace her, then abruptly stop three feet away, freeze, and put his arm forward, his palm out signaling "stop" to her. Disorganized-attachment children often freeze, not knowing what to do, what will come next, what they want, what their mothers want.

This may be all too complicated for the courts, but when I describe this research, I see the judges sit forward, wanting to learn. Everyone in the courtroom seems to go silent. They start remembering their own mothers. They think about their own parenting. They wonder how they or their children would be categorized.

During the home visit or in my office, I play around with separations and reunions, and observe how the child reacts. It's not officially the Strange Situation, but I might ask a mother to go to the laundry room in the basement for a minute and close the door behind her when she leaves. Then I look to see if the child toddles over to the door waiting for her to emerge, cries, or goes on doing exactly what he's been doing. The expected response will be different depending on the age and context. While there are hundreds of thousands of research articles on attachment, for the most part confirming how important it is, there are very few that tell a psychologist what to look for in the older child. I use an established list of behaviors and watch for the positive ones, the exchange of smiles, the sharing of attention, the hugs hello and goodbye, the small touches between mother and child, the leaning into a snuggle, the child bringing things to the mom or dad to consider. And I notice the negative signs, the child playing with his back turned to his mother for such a long time, the little girl pulling away from a hug, the preschooler showing some kind of can't-get-enough-of-you confusion in a moment, or anger expressed towards the primary caregiver in words or body language: "You *never* bring the right snack!"

I have to ask myself, though, how can a child who has been placed in foster care possibly be secure? DCF has moved the child, placed her with new parents temporarily, and eighteen months later I'm supposed to see signs that the child is securely attached to the first mother? Depending on her age and early experiences, she could possibly be securely attached—not to her first mother but to the second set of parents she has stayed with. If I were that child and someone tried to move me again, I'd fight like mad to stay where I was.

So I focus on the mothers more than the children. Upon arriving for a visit, a child offers the mother a Valentine's card that says "I love you" in glitter. "It's homemade!" he says. And his mother, heart-breakingly, doesn't take it from his hands or exclaim at its beauty. Instead, she says, "Hold onto it. I'll look at it later," but forgets about it. Another child trips over a shark puppet left on the floor of my office and falls. She stands, whimpers, and brings her finger over to her mother to kiss it, saying she has an "owey." Her mother kisses the finger and then looks at me and mocks her, saying out loud, "What a drama queen!"

These are mothers who cannot stand for their children to want them, to need them. In attachment terms, it brings to mind for them, to the unconscious mind, their own unreliable mothers. It agitates them. They want the need to go away. Need means vulnerability, and vulnerability needs to be smushed like an ant on the kitchen counter before it reaches the spilled sugar.

I understand the avoidant children best. I tend towards taking care of myself when I need someone else, denying my need for another. Am I avoidantly attached? I do not visit my mother's gravesite, the mausoleum, actually, where she was not exactly "buried" because she was afraid to be underground and we respected that wish, in spite of our understanding that dead people are not aware of their surroundings. But we also were aware that my mother had a peasant mother, the grandmother we all had grown up with in our home, with her old country superstitions, spitting three times to ward off evil.

I think I was close to my mother once. But my pleasure at my mother's ability to draw a picture of a simple but beautiful princess when I was three or four gave way to disdain for the things she didn't know how to do when I got older. What also grew was my frustration at her strictness and her unwillingness to examine reasons when making judgments about what I was and was not allowed to do. One couldn't present reasonable arguments to her without making her feel dumb and then feeling guilty for doing so. As my dad knew he was smarter than my mother, so did I begin to feel superior.

After about eight or nine years old, I avoided my mother, choosing to be more like my competent father, who told me he knew everything and who had power and punch, like the no-filter Camels he chain-smoked, four packs a day. I grew up competent like my dad, but maybe I held onto what attachment theorists call an "internal working model" of that earlier mother. Not the mother who grew smaller in voice and who hid at home in the suburbs, inadequate to the tasks of suburban living as she didn't drive, didn't work, didn't make friends with the neighborhood women, and didn't know how to cook.

The mother of my earlier childhood in the poor neighborhood around Wilson Ave., an area of Chicago called Uptown, hustled her three children into buses to go to the doctor and then hustled us into small hot dog shops where we all sat in a row at the counter for a treat afterward. That early mother stood up to my father, throwing the frog ashtray at him and breaking it in one of my most vivid childhood memories. I liked to fall asleep in that mother's bed, before my father joined her later at night. An insomniac, when he came to bed at two or three in the morning, he would walk me back to my own bedroom that I shared with my sister. At a pretty late age, I stopped sleeping with the mother I had already begun to disdain during the day. But that child, the one who still slept next to her mother at night, I know now is an attached child, one who is soothed by the body of the early mother if not by the unreasonable mother she argued with in daylight. The avoidantly attached child is still attached. Make no error on that score. Sometime in her childhood, though, she begins to think it's not okay to need, that it's better to be able to take care of yourself, to turn off that longing. The need, however, remains.

2. A CHILD IN THE SANDBOX

The seven-year-old girl with long blond hair and a daisy headband comes into my office and walks to the right, which is the side of the office with all the toys. She doesn't flop down on the furry beanbag chair but walks the perimeter, inspecting. "Are there any evils here? Do you have any evils?" I guess at what she means and move to the dolls, holding up one that is supposed to look like the wicked queen in *Snow White* but is bedraggled, hair sticking straight out as if struck by lightning in a cartoon, and half-dressed. I grab my shark puppet along the way. "Is this what you're looking for?"

"I love horses. Did you know that? Can you get me some of those?" I help her collect all the horses in the room. It's amazing how many horses I can find in my therapy room once I've put my mind to it. There are the Playmobil horses from the Native American set gathering cobwebs in the corner; the unbending horses from the Medieval Knights set; the horse family nestled in among the kangaroo, lion, and tiger families; and stray small horses among the miniatures on display next to the sandbox.

Julie sets the horses up in my sandbox, a plastic makeshift version of a sand tray for sandtray therapy. Sandtray therapy was first developed by Margaret Lowenfeld, who opened a clinic for "difficult" children in England. It was taken up by the Jungian analyst Dora Kalff, who taught therapists to use the sandtray to understand the internal symbols of a child's world, the preverbal and lost meanings. The sandtray therapist collects miniatures and lines them up on shelves near a sandtray, or two sandtrays, one for wet sand, one for dry. As with all play therapy, the premise is that children heal themselves through play. In Jungian sandtray therapy, opposites are explored—above the sand/underneath it, good vs. evil—and archetypes from mythology, fairy tales, and popular culture find themselves posed in relation to one another in complicated ways: Moses gives Mickey Mouse a piggyback ride. A witch and a ballerina are in a small rowboat. Among my miniatures are a skeleton, a wizard, a fairy godmother, an orangutan mother with a baby on her back, soldiers, farmers, all kinds of sea animals, Moses (who is sometimes mistaken for God), a ballerina, a witch, knights, and a gas station attendant, as well as boats, blocks, seashells, a phone booth, and fences.

Julie puts all the horses on one side of the sandbox and sets up a fence around them. "Every snake is everywhere," she says. This statement might say it all. I take her literally for now and gather the snake miniatures in a pile next to her.

The horses, she tells me, are a family and they are afraid of snakes. "The horses don't want to run into an anaconda," she states ominously.

I ask, "Have you ever seen an anaconda?" detaching my talk from the play and moving it into a present conversation, something I teach my students never to do.

"No, that would give me a nightmare."

"Oh, and do you have nightmares?"

"Lots of them. Even when I pray."

"Praying helps?"

"If praying doesn't, I don't know what does. . . . Maybe screaming."

Julie moves some lions to the outside edge of the sandbox and pauses, staring ahead. Then with a large sigh she breathes out, "No matter what, they're dead." At this thought, she gets up and goes to the dollhouse, and I follow, knees cracking as I get up from the floor.

At the dollhouse I can ask some attachment questions for the evaluation. I put a little girl in a small, wooden bed upstairs and say to Julie, "Let's pretend this is a little girl and she's been asleep. It's the middle of the night and she wakes up from a nightmare. What do you think she'll do?" I've put a mother doll downstairs in a wooden armchair in front of a black screen of a wooden TV. Sitting stiffly, staring at the blank screen like that, she looks traumatized. I want to see if the little girl calls for her mother.

"She lies there—thinking."

"She lies there thinking," I reflect back. "Is the little girl frightened?"

"Yes."

"What is she thinking about?"

"Nothing. She likes the dark. I used to be afraid of the dark. I used to think spiders were going to attack me and eat me. Like snakes. I like snakes now." After admitting the girl is frightened, she turns it around to say she isn't. She is in control. She likes snakes, the dark.

Some children make the doll who wakes up in the middle of the night get herself a glass of water, turn on the light, and play a little game in bed until she falls back asleep. This doll takes care of herself when she's afraid. Some children have the doll call out to a mother who doesn't come upstairs. When I ask what happens after the little girl cries out, they might have the mother doll yell upstairs, "Go back to sleep!" Some children become agitated by the question and have the doll do silly things like climb out the window and play on the roof. A child who cannot call out to her mother is in danger. Perhaps putting oneself in danger is the only way to get the mother to come.

A child crying out in the middle of the night, one who needs comfort, who needs me to curl up at the foot of his bed and make the world safe again—what bliss. How I wish I could provide comfort like that again. But maybe I dwelled too long at the foot of the bed. Maybe I should have rested for only five or ten minutes and told Willy, "You'll be all right," and left him to discover that he would be all right, with me in the next room. Are we always titrating mother-love? Is it too much? Too little? Does anyone get this right?

Julie is in attachment therapy with Fern, her foster mother, a woman who has no intention of adopting her. I asked the therapist earlier, on the phone, why he is doing this work to get Julie to attach to Fern if Julie will eventually lose her? Won't that loss be even more traumatic? He answers that the capacity to attach is what he is hoping Julie will achieve with this therapy, and if accomplished, she will be able to see any caregiver as a potentially reliable source of security and comfort. He believes attachments can be transferable, to the next foster home, and the next, and even an adoptive home. I'm not sure about that.

Such is life. We teach children to attach and then they must bear loss, and if they're strong enough, they withstand loss. Better to have loved and lost . . .

Julie has what DCF social workers call an "attachment disorder." Some DCF workers like to talk about a "reactive attachment disorder," an overused diagnosis that, in reality, is rare. Using it for every attachment problem is wrong and problematic in so many ways. A diagnosis sounds more important and less vague than an attachment category, but I prefer to use the phrase "insecurely attached." But what kind? Considering the attachment categories, Julie seems more avoidantly attached in her play than disorganized. She is fearful (every snake is everywhere) but has to take care of her fears herself. She is demoralized (everything dies) and that comes from the loss. She is also distant and detached, which is a good way to protect herself from loss.

Julie turns her back to the dollhouse and eyes the basket of puppets. She says to me in earnest, "I was thinking of a very bad idea."

"Yes?" I ask, leaning forward. I am thrilled when a child makes her inner life open to me.

"I was thinking that I was in the ocean and I took that stuffed animal with me." She points to the shark puppet. "If I did that, then the sharks might come and think it's a baby shark and not notice it wasn't a real one because it doesn't blink. It doesn't move."

In this story, like "snakes are everywhere," sharks are everywhere and come alive for a moment in her vigilant stance. Or maybe they are only somewhat alive. Baby sharks freeze; they don't blink. I don't understand this story yet. If the baby shark doesn't blink, then would the other sharks swim by and miss it? Or is the point that the other sharks would be near the baby shark, hold the fake baby shark and treat her as one of them? Before I can ask, Julie has moved on.

"Hallo, Guvnor! Would you like some of my nice tarts I'm selling today?"

I laugh unexpectedly and she smiles back at me. Our eyes meet and I feel the connection. Where the hell did that jolly British voice come from?

"Why yes, m'lady, I'd like a pear tart to serve to the duke and duchess tonight."

She and I go on talking in exaggerated British accents, and she is quite good at it. We are warmly attaching as we role-play other people from another country, fake people I am thinking, like the fake baby shark.

And that very well may be the way Julie attaches to a foster mother, playing at being a daughter to the foster mother's playing at being a mom. This play can grow into trust, if this false self is not too successful, if when the baby shark blinks or even bites, the foster mother holds the little fish and welcomes her anger, labeling it as it is. You are angry, baby shark. Oh Julie, you have a lot to be angry about.

I hear steps on the winding staircase up to my office. Julie's birth mother is coming up the stairs unbidden from the waiting room below for her part of the visit. It's time and I am going to observe them together. But before I allow her mother into this play space pulsing with possibilities, I give Julie some control over the observation part of the session fast approaching. I ask her if she wants a short or a long goodbye with her mother when the time comes. She says, "No."

3. ADOPTION

When I was eight years old, my mother went through her cedar chest, a sacred locked chest that smelled wonderful when opened and contained diaries, photos, linen, old magazines, and more. She was doing this for me, looking for my birth certificate because I demanded to see it. I was hoping to discover that I was adopted and that my real parents, somewhere far off, preferably in a castle, were beautiful and good and kind and that someday I would find them.

In a country and culture where myths of "real" parents run deep, adoption is a problem. And although I desperately wished for it at one time in my own childhood, adopted children live unconsciously with a fantasy that the good parents, the real ones, the ones who represent pure love and connection are out there somewhere.

"Real" of course is the wrong word. The real parent is the one who raised you. Paul is Willy's "real" parent although he met Willy when Willy already was fifteen months old. There are many configurations of "real" parents in the world, from grandparents, aunts and uncles, adoptive parents, and the parents who raise you to chosen parents who are mentors, coaches, teachers, neighbors. The "real" parent is the one who wakes up at night and worries about you.

At nine I ran away from home. I didn't pack anything. I just wrote a note and left, imagining I would eventually live in the woods with a friendly bear and eat berries to survive. Old enough to know this probably wouldn't work out, I'm sure persistence and stubbornness blocked that knowing from awareness as I stomped down the alley where my townhouse was, situated along a chain of red and beige brick townhouses. By the time I had reached the end of the alley, I wasn't sure which way to go, so I circled to the right and found my way to the street parallel to the alley. Having committed myself to running away, I paused there, not knowing what would happen next. As the sky turned a poignant pink and purple, I thought I would probably need to wait until the morning to figure out how to get to those woods. I was a city girl then, as I am at heart now, even though I live at the edge of acres of woods. At that age I didn't know if there even were any woods in Chicago. But if there were, they were probably not the kind of woods that have thatched huts with dwarves and wishing wells.

I reached the point at which the parallel street met the curved beginning of the alley that I lived off of. But there, at the end of the alley, marching in horizontal formation, were my mother, sister, and brother. Seen, I turned and ran in the other direction, my heart racing. I popped into the backyard of the bungalow that had a swing set in the backyard, a wonderful thing in those days to have a swing set of one's own. So spectacular was that swing set that all the townhouse kids on the other side of the alley couldn't resist using it. We would swing on the swings and hang out chatting at the top of the slide. We were swing-set-less urchins and not very nice to her daughter, so Mrs. Diamond would chase us off it and out of her backyard, but we would return. How entitled we felt to someone else's property. I still marvel at that.

I peeped out the back of the Diamonds' yard and into the alley, and there they were again. They had seen me turn in and were walking, marching, towards my retreat.

It was almost dark and something weird was happening to my thinking. Emerging quite slowly was the realization that there were no woods. And like a psychotic person with a delusion, who has a moment of questioning before incorporating the newfound reality into her delusion, I was at a loss for what would happen next.

I heard grown men shout to each other calling me "she" and "her," the fathers, working fathers who never had time for children. The lights from their flashlights scanned the grass up to the tops of the trees, crisscrossing. I wanted to show myself, but now too much of a fuss had been made, and I would be deeply ashamed of my failure. I could never tell them I wanted to go to the woods. That would sound so childish. I knew already that their interpretation would be that I was spoiled and had done this "for attention." Everything those days was said to be done "for attention."

I slipped between two houses and found a hole in the ground alongside the back of a fancier home, one of those wells made so that light can reach the basement. It was deep, but I tried to ease myself down, hurting my knees when I fell on them. My butt on the cold white stones, I began convincing myself that I could spend the night there. I could just fall asleep and leave in the morning, looking for something, somewhere, but probably not woods.

Then a flashlight lit on me. I gazed up and a crowd of men were looking down at me in the hole. Arms reached down. I was lifted out roughly and brought out to my mother, brother, and sister. There was my father, too, and then I saw my grandmother who instantly crumpled, fainting at the sight of me. I had forgotten about her. I loved my grandmother so much. When she was conscious again and standing, the attention turned back to me, and my family marched me home through a throng of angry neighborhood men. The neighborhood mothers had their own children back in bed. "You should spank her good," said one. "You're in for it now," said another. The adults were furious and gleeful, and I was ashamed to be crying in front of them.

When we got home, my father sat me on the couch while my grandmother, mother, sister, and brother watched and listened. He said that everyone had been telling him to spank me, but he wasn't going to do that. He knew that something was bothering me, and he wanted to know what. I didn't know any more what I was so bothered by earlier in the evening. I had wanted to say something to my parents, but they had been too busy talking to other grownups and shooed me away from their closed circle of lawn chairs. They had been sitting with neighbors, smoking, talking, and I had been mad. Some boy had mistreated me I think. Called me a name. I'd been outraged that I needed them, and they didn't come out of the circle to talk to me. It was intolerable to sit in my empty room alone with my tears.

My mother is a blur in this memory. My grandmother, from the old country, I recall soaked with sweat and worry. My father searched to understand why I would do something so serious as running away. I didn't have the words to tell him that it wasn't so serious. It was a moment's decision that once taken I had to commit to. In this story and in memory, my mother belongs to my siblings, my sister and brother who marched with her down the alley to find me. I belonged to my father. And to another mother, an "othermother," my grandmother.

I had some bad experiences in my childhood, but I don't have a lasting childhood trauma, one that you feel in your bones and that you revisit again and again. I don't believe Willy has one either. I grew up with a father and a mother. One took, the other didn't. That may be true for Willy as well. But I do know that whatever my failures, I listened to Willy intensely, allowing any interruption to my conversations with adults, responding to most needs, ready to search the pantry for another snack when the first one was rejected, and ready to hear what he had to say. So why did he hide? Did it start as a whim he needed to commit to? Why did he start a search for woods and bears and berries? Why disappear into a hole outside the house, hoping we would not find him?

4. MIRRORING

Willy, as a boy, never ran away, but he had a propensity for getting lost, pushing far ahead of me and then losing his bearings. It was as if getting lost was a test of me as much as it was a test of his ability to manage without me. Would I find him? I could see he loved the freedom of venturing out on his own, riding his bike all over a new neighborhood, movement, speed. When he returned from being lost, he was amazed that I hadn't even realized he'd been gone. His five minutes of frantic searching for me on a bike in the snaking streets of a development in Wisconsin when we were visiting an old college friend of mine were not mirrored by my own five minutes of frantic searching for him. His running up and down the aisles of the botanical garden was not matched by my running up and down the aisles. I didn't know he was lost.

What does the good enough mother do? What does she know? Does she know what her child feels before he feels it? Does she know it when he feels it? Or is it good enough to mirror it when he expresses it. When the child returns and states, "I was lost," is she responsible for knowing the depth of the panic he must have felt and pull him close against her? Or does she wait and watch to see if he needs her? When, hours later, he says, "I was really scared," does she then pull him close? Or does she mock him and say, "It was a small museum. We would have found you." Does she reflect, "That must have felt terrible"? Or does she apologize, "I should have been looking for you"? Does she explain what he could have done differently: "You could have mapped the streets in your mind or only taken right turns as you rode your bike," hoping to instill confidence in himself for the next time? Or does she ask, "What did you do to find your way back?" and praise him, "Look how you found your way back!" He might reply, "But I was so scared." She might mirror back, "You were so scared."

For almost a hundred years, therapists and analysts have described, in various forms, the responsiveness of the mother to the child as "mirroring." The psychoanalyst Heinz Kohut wrote that the development of the self depended on two processes: mirroring and idealization. Mirroring occurs when the mother, or caregiver, reflects back to the baby all of his wonderfulness and in so doing creates a nascent self, the first bud of a self, and later a grandiose self in the best sense of the word "grandiose": "I am here. I am wonderful. I am powerful." Without this more positive version, grandiosity becomes an automatic defensive reaction to hurt or insult, a narcissistic defense we see in politicians and other powerful people. Feeling small and insignificant, these figures prop themselves up by reasserting their invulnerability and superiority.

D. W. Winnicott, trained by the psychoanalyst Melanie Klein, came from a different school of thought from Kohut, called Object Relations. He was a pediatrician before becoming an analyst and described the mother as a "holding environment." While Klein thought infants start life broken in two, "schizoid," later becoming depressed by their own ambivalence towards their mother, Winnicott proposed that the real mother and not the baby's fantasy of his mother was important. The real mother only needed to be "good enough," getting it right most of the time. She needn't be perfect. The good enough mother mirrors the baby when he needs mirroring and allows him to go on being when he doesn't. Through mirroring, the good enough mother brings the baby into being. His first self is reflected by her into being. Then later, when she allows him his separateness, allows him to "go on being" and doesn't intrude into that space, she gives him the opportunity to develop creative thought and to understand that even when she isn't reflecting him, he exists. He is all right.

Mirroring produces mind-mindedness, the ability to understand what is going on in another person's mind. After the emergence of what is called "theory of mind" research, the British psychoanalysts Peter Fonagy and Mary Target, of University College London, wrote that good enough parenting depended on parents being able to understand what was in the minds of their children. The mind-mindedness of mothers indeed predicts how well a child can complete the cognitive tasks of theory of mind researchers at age four.

I mind-minded Willy to death as a baby. "You're sad now. You want that red car very much and you're sad that mommy won't buy it. You're mad at mommy right now." No wonder he became a sphinx. Did I mind-mind him into a hidey-hole? Into a place where his insides could not be seen? Did my watchfulness create an unease that needed soothing with drugs? Was his introverted silent response a way to develop his own person, a person who can't be seen by me?

Or does he want me to chase him? All the way to France I will later fly, in a panic, to rescue him from a relapse, lost and frightened myself. Like the mother in Margaret Wise Brown's 1942 book

The Runaway Bunny. "If you become a fish in a trout stream, said his mother, I will become a fisherman and fish for you"—the theme of my mothering. When the bunny becomes a crocus in a hidden garden, his mother becomes a gardener. When he becomes a bird and flies away, she becomes a tree for him to land in. He becomes a sailboat and she becomes a wind that blows him where *she* wants him to go. I returned to this book recently when a friend shocked me by saying she hated this beloved standard. "Give the bunny some independence to explore the world," my friend said. "What an intrusive mother!"

When a son hides, is it an invitation to chase him? He might be lost, in a panic, or he might be a crocus in a garden, laying down roots, waiting for me to pass by and reflect, What a beautiful flower. My phone calls went unanswered. When I saw him he was thin and drawn. Were those silences really invitations?—to show up at his door? to feed him? Or was I supposed to let him learn he could go on being and feed himself?

5. RELAPSE

Under normal circumstances, a trip through Paris and down to the Riviera would excite me—the beaches, palm trees, sidewalk cafes that serve sandwiches on miniature baguettes, the shopping and museums, and the long walks past stunning architecture. This is how I recall the trip to Nice to be with Willy after his French girlfriend with an Irish name, Eileen, saved his life.

First there was a text from Eileen saying that Willy had been in the hospital from an overdose and was now home again, home being their apartment in Nice. Then there was a call from Willy: "I'm okay. I had a relapse."

"Do you want me to come?"

"No, you don't have to."

"Would it help?"

Silence again. "Yes, come."

Does he need me? Does he need my money? Is money security? Is it love?

"Should I come today? Right now? Or will you be safe if I teach my class tomorrow and then fly out the next day? Tell me the truth." Already I'm on the internet looking at the costs of flights. They are expensive. Anything for Willy if it will keep him alive, but my responsibility to my teaching nags at me. It ends up being fine with him that I come to Nice a little later, after my class. I call Paul to let him know everything. It is expensive, so he will stay in Vermont and I will go to Nice alone. Somehow again, I need to bustle around while at the same time I need Paul to stay put. My safe harbor.

I have been learning French as I drive the long stretch of highway to my job in Boston—the Pimsleur approach. It promises French for conversation, but it is no help to me in the cab from the airport in Nice. I don't understand the driver, and he doesn't understand me. Still, I protest the cost as a way to protest this whole trip before reaching Willy. I didn't cause it; I can't control it; I can't cure it—the 3 Cs that Al-Anon family members repeat to each other. But there are some things I think I can control. "I will give you thirty euros." The driver, however, wants fifty and tells me, "This is what it costs," and I pay. I feel cheated. I am no good except to pay for things, and yet it was a relief to have a little argument just then.

Willy greets me outside his apartment building and takes me through an alley between two modern white concrete buildings that leads to a set of stairs to a courtyard that has a faded pastel-colored, plastic Big Wheel in the path, and then to another set of stairs to a fifth-floor apartment. Even the apartment has two floors, one room on top of another. My knees hurt. I want to hear everything, and I also want to sleep.

Eileen tells me the details, and Willy pipes in to make her details less frightening. He went out for a stroll, and while he was out he passed a hospital emergency center. The doors were wide open. People were busy inside, and he simply walked in and looked around. He spied a closet where medication was kept and stepped into it, quickly grabbing any drugs, guessing at the French names of ones that would serve. And then he quickly stepped out into the street again and found a place to take them, on the steps down to the beach. Back home that evening, according to Eileen, he was acting weird and then he was hard asleep, and she couldn't wake him up. She couldn't hear his heartbeat. She couldn't feel it. Who knows how to feel a pulse? She called 112, and when the ambulance arrived, the emergency team took him on a stretcher down the five flights of stairs, across the courtyard, down the next flight, through the alleyway into an ambulance with the two-toned siren. They pumped his stomach and gave him an injection of something to counteract the pills' effects. Maybe it was naltrexone. Does it matter? I can't stand to know those details, and even when I learn them, I forget them. I hate drugs. But he's alive. He is here in front of me. He is Willy, himself.

The next day we walk along the streets of Nice, a gentle, sunny day, palm tree trunks stiff but their leaves are swaying. We then walk along the beach. It is windy and the strip of sand is set across the boulevard, just steps away from the magnificent casinos with art deco facades. For gamblers, they are grand invitations to come inside. I have no desire to enter a casino, but remember that as a girl I imagined myself as the woman in the red slinky dress who blew on a handsome man's dice to give him luck. I don't feel lucky anymore.

We walk to a neighborhood with fancy white houses, small green parks, and large marble buildings of important and historic associations. I ask questions and Willy, grateful that I have come, wants to answer them. Like a mussel after three minutes in the pot, the shock has forced him open, and I take advantage of it, asking "petit" questions that lead up to the big questions. As we walk peacefully, I am careful not to overwhelm him and pace my questions like the well-spaced palm trees along the road.

I don't know why he asks me what I know about Jesus. It's October after all and there are no Christmas decorations yet. But grand churches are everywhere, standing as monuments to a story that neither of us knows well. He knows very little about Jesus because we are Jewish and because he is not much of a reader. I'm guilty of not forcing him to read every night and for allowing the TV and video games after school and even in the evening. Now my son doesn't even know the "greatest story ever told" or, if not the great-est story, the one that is echoed in so many of the superhero movies he's watched.

I tell him what I know from reading novels, going to friends' churches, singing in choruses, weddings, looking at art, and from my two-part college course called "The Bible as Literature." As it turns out, I don't know very much.

There are four gospels, I tell him, and they all relate the same story, only the last one is kind of wild and into the future and makes the claim that there will be an apocalypse but good people will be saved, just swooped up on the spot, in something called "the rap-ture." Is this true or am I filling in based on TV?

God decides to have a son, but I don't for the life of me know why. I think it is to save the human race because we've been bad, and certainly that makes sense. And so he chooses Mary to have this son, but I don't know why her. Mary is married to Joseph. This I am sure of. God sends an angel. It feels like my last chance as a mother to teach and inform, and yet I am not sure who. I think it is Michael. But Michael is a saint I know, from working at St. Michael's Col-lege, so how can he be an angel? I can picture a da Vinci painting called *Annunciation* and a little cherub is whispering in Mary's ear to impregnate her. But am I imagining this whisper? An announcement is more formal than a whisper, something requiring trumpets.

I check to see if Willy is listening and he wants me to go on, to just talk as we walk. So I skip to the part where Mary's about ready to give birth, and she and Joseph go to several inns and face many an innkeeper who turns them away. I picture Joseph and Mary as five-year-olds in a Christmas play as I tell the story. Then there's "away in a manger, no crib for a bed," suggesting to me that one innkeeper let them sleep in his manger. Decades of choral singing for Christmas concerts has filled me in. Mary gives birth to the baby there, and she names him Jesus. "Remember Christ our Savior was born on Christ-mas Day," goes one carol, but of course he wasn't born on Christmas Day. Three wise men bring gifts from afar, on three ships that come "a'sailing in." These wise men most likely already know that he's the son of God or why would they bring gifts: frankincense, myrrh, and, crap, what was the third one?

Having never sung at Easter, I move quickly through the next part. Jesus lives and is a carpenter and does a bunch of miracles, and there's another Mary who is a prostitute and I'm not sure why she starts to hang around with him but he saves her. From what? From prostitution? I think he just extends love and doesn't judge her. Is that how she's saved, how we're all saved?

And Jesus turns something into fish for the hungry and water into wine for the thirsty. He says, "Turn the other cheek," as advice on how to treat those who harm you. And basically he has a message of forgiveness. He gains a big following, and then there was some trumped-up charge of thievery.

Jesus will later say, "Judas, why have you forsaken me?" No, that doesn't sound right. He will say, "God, why have you forsaken me?" when he is on the cross. He has a moment of doubt, like Doubting Thomas, one of the disciples. Does he say anything to Judas at all? Judas betrayed him, but what does he say? "Et tu, Judas?" Let's skip Judas.

So Jesus is on the cross, nailed to it, and he dies and is buried in a cave, although I'm not sure why a cave. I don't know what happens next, but I know as an absolute fact "a child is risen," he is risen, or arisen? He appears to Mary or to his disciples and claims he is born again, and that he really is the Son of God sent to earth. So, the conclusion of the story is, if you believe in him, you will be saved. You will have eternal life in heaven, with him, with God, with angels, and, if you're Catholic, I think with saints too.

How does the story end for his mother Mary? Mary wept. I remember that line from a song. Or was it Jesus wept? I prefer Mary wept. She accepted that she was powerless to change what she could not change and all the power lay with her son. She had to allow him to go on being. Support his going on being, however supernatural a being he was.

Willy listens, bemused. I am aware that I do not sound at all like a college professor. We stop in at the Suboxone clinic that he can only go to every three days because they need safeguards against abuse. Oh France, where the clinic for addicts rests comfortably amid marble mansions. The French addicts in the waiting room are a combination of young and hip and old and worn. Willy asks the doctor to give him a two-week supply that will last him until he can connect to a clinic in Massachusetts, where I will be taking him. The doctor believes him, as he should. After all, his mother is in the waiting room. I pay twenty dollars for the two-week supply knowing this would cost so much more in many states in the US.

Back at his apartment in Nice, we pack up his things, his pregnant girlfriend with the Irish name, their two stray cats whose airline tickets I have also bought, and his guitar. The night before we leave we watch *The Matrix* on TV with subtitles in French for Eileen, a movie I had never seen before. I can't follow the plot, although I note a resurrection after three days. And I don't understand what's going on with this red pill. I don't want to think about pills. We get on our separate trains and planes the next day to meet in Boston, where the person I usually stay with when I work in Boston will say "no room at the inn," and my friends Doug and Ricardo will open their home to Eileen and Willy following some discussion that it's the Christian thing to do. Willy will start his third round of treatment in Massachusetts. So he was rescued. Will he be saved?

6. OTHER MOTHERS

Social workers save lives. They are the steadfast new mothers to mothers in trouble, mothers who are in search of role models, or nurturing, or praise, or mirroring. They often suffer for the sins of these earlier mothers.

On a hot Friday afternoon in August, after seeing a mother who had relapsed, Lara Sobel, a social worker, left the Barre DCF office. She had just had an intimate conversation with a young mother who initially had been afraid of the tall, slim social worker, her power, her possible judgments, but who eventually relaxed when Lara told her she believed that relapse is part of the process, that Lara was going to help this mother get back on her feet and get her children back.

When Lara left the DCF office that day, she may have been thinking "two more weeks until vacation." Maybe she was hoping her husband had made dinner. She could have been about to pick up her two daughters from a summer arts camp. Jody Herring, however, was waiting outside in the parking lot and shot her straight on, twice, with a .270-caliber, bolt-action Remington rifle.

State's attorney Scott Williams, running on a treadmill in a gym across the parking lot, heard the shots, hopped off, and arrived at the scene amazingly in time to tackle Jody Herring to the ground. He then moved to Lara and held her in his arms as they waited for the ambulance to arrive, his body absorbing the adrenaline rush, hers weakening until she died. Another state's attorney, Gregory McNaughton, also happened to be nearby and had sprinted across the parking lot and took hold of Herring's arm to keep her there. It would seem that the parking lots of Barre are awash with lawyers.

I haven't been to the Barre DCF office, so in my mind I picture the red brick of another state government office in another Vermont town. These buildings pretty much look alike, constructed in an era when official buildings were made of brick and homes were wood, government set to stay put for the long haul but families left to weather termites, floods, and fire. In this other office, two weeks earlier, I interviewed a father who had threatened to kill his DCF worker. I knew about that threat before I met the father, but it didn't occur to me to worry for my own safety. I briefly considered it but asked myself, Why would he want to kill me? I was somebody who might end up advocating for the return of his children. On the other hand, a dad who threatens to kill is probably not going to get his kids back.

In the middle of my interview with this father at the DCF office I asked him point-blank, "Did you threaten to kill your DCF worker?"

"I sure did, and I meant it. He's an ass."

"But did you really mean it?"

He smiled and squinted, "I probably wouldn'ta killed him, but I woulda made him need to go to the hospital."

I smiled back. "Are you really saying this to me? Do you mean that?"

A smile can work. "Well, I wouldn'ta hurt him. I woulda just laid him out."

"What does 'laid him out' mean?"

"You know, lay him out. He wouldn't mess with me again." Still smiling.

I stopped talking him down notch by notch once I got the feeling that he was all talk and strutting his masculinity, showing me his control of a situation where another man had all the control. He probably wasn't going to kill his worker, but who knows? Most parents aren't going to kill their workers, but then one does.

Two weeks later, I studied in the *Free Press* the rainbow-glazed photo of Lara Sobel that journalists had, during the first days after her death, stolen off Facebook, a photo that placed her beside her husband and her two daughters, about nine and twelve. All that summer, the rainbow tint on photos, like the gels put over theatre spotlights, had indicated support for the passing of the gay marriage bill, lovely to see on a photo so heterotypical. Father, mother, two children. Looking at the photo, one could guess about her life after graduation from the University of Vermont's School of Social Work, a marriage to a farmer or another UVM grad student, the birth of her first daughter, a move to the country, gardening, tomatoes and too many zucchinis she brought into the office to give away in late August, placing them next to the other zucchinis brought in, a dog, a big one, that roamed their property unleashed, the birth of her second daughter, daycare, so hard to arrange, kindergarten, summer camps, vacations. Smiling in her wide-brimmed hat in the photo, her husband and daughters next to her, she was clearly on vacation.

She wasn't the only victim. On the day of the murder, Jody Herring had called her cousin Ronda, who had played the all-important role of "collateral contact" in the state's evaluation of Jody's parenting.

Jody left a message: "You guys need to stop calling DCF unless you guys are going to have it coming to you." What a strange threat considering that Jody had already lost her nine-year-old daughter a month earlier. Why would her family continue to call DCF, or was she remembering the time in the past when they did so, out of concern for her daughter? In another call to her brother that day, Jody left the message: "If you think anything of your sister, you'll get a hold of me now or ASAP." That was her first message to him, a cry for help two hours before the killing. But then there was another message, "Watch the news." It ended with a warning: "Watch the news and you'll wish you got ahold of me earlier." She had given her brother four minutes to stop her. Jody's brother is still alive, but her cousin, her cousin's mother, and her sister are all dead. She was charged with their murders too.

A year earlier, in 2014, two toddlers, Dezirae Sheldon and Peighton Geraw, died in the custody of their mothers, after which Vermont DCF began placing more and more children in custody earlier. Since then, most of the 33 percent increase in children placed in custody had to do with parents who were addicted to opiates. The result of this change of policy might have been that more parents got treatment. Or they may have received other kinds of therapy or medication to address depression or anxiety. They were asked to get urine screens at random times that their worker called them, to travel to official sites where a staff person watches to make sure an addict does not sneak in a baggie of someone else's urine. These parents were given a chance and yet we know now, with all these services, it would still be incredibly hard for them to stop.

I've seen DCF workers who were full of compassion and connected to the addicted mothers they work with, but also some who were stand-offish or even hostile. They are mothers of a kind to their clients, othermothers, and the transference and countertransference feelings are intense. That means that their clients will displace onto them all sorts of feelings they have for their own mothers. They must contain all sorts of longing and then a whole lot of rage. And the workers will have to check their inclinations to become whatever mother they had or want to be, too distant, too involved, too responsive, too punishing.

For my own reasons, I am sympathetic to the addicted moms, trying but failing, wistfully loving their children but mightily loving the high. I innocently believe that my own experience and empathy protects me from their anger, but clearly that is magical thinking. Still, I believe that if I care and stay connected to the human being before me, that the human being before me will connect back. That is a good reflection of my attachment history, the belief that the world is fundamentally safe and that everyone can receive love if it is given. And yet, somehow, that sounds a bit naive.

7. A MOTHER WITH NO OTHERS

Sometimes I like a mother a little too much. Liking her or not liking her is unprofessional, but I can see this tendency in other psychologists' reports too, the liking and not liking. A psychologist might soften the wording in his report, remembering that the mother he liked would read the report. He might write in a way that suggests more hope for the future than he believes is possible, given what he learned of her past trauma. He might have fudged his recommendations to give her one last chance.

Charmaine's hoop earrings hung low and touched her shoulders. I would be the first psychologist to evaluate this young mother originally from Birmingham, Alabama, a woman with a nice sense of fashion, sitting on my old-fashioned couch.

It was winter, the sad part of a Vermont winter, the part that comes after the first snow, after the first sledding, after the Christmas and New Year's parties, the part of winter that stretches ahead hostile and unending like so many of the country roads. Vermonters wear big boots with rubber soles. But Charmaine wore trendy boots with heels, buckles, and straps, perhaps enjoying, even celebrating the Vermont winter as I did my first year. Wait till next year, said more than one neighbor.

Charmaine's lawyer called on me to help explain this woman to DCF and to the court. I was asked to be on the mother's side and ignore the infant, for now. But I never can do that, even though this young mother seemed to be practically a child herself. Some can, but I can't.

Some psychologists formulate opinions they are paid to form. But if a parent's lawyer hires them, and the psychologist writes an opinion that the parent's lawyer doesn't like, the lawyer can simply not use that opinion. This only works, however, if the other side doesn't know about the evaluation and report. If the report would be damaging or unhelpful, the lawyer doesn't have to use it, and the psychologist is not permitted, legally, to talk about or share her report. It can be as if the report never existed, if nobody knows the psychologist was hired. Some of the time, the psychologist doesn't need to even write up the report. She performs the evaluation and then tells the lawyer what she thinks she is going to write, and he says, "Okay. There's no need to write this one up. Thank you for your service." He gets off the phone quickly after reminding the psychologist about confidentiality. This happened once when a lawyer of a possible sex offender had me watch the video of the police interview with the child. I watched the child make her tentative disclosure to the police and believed her. That was good information for this man's lawyer. If after watching the recording I believed her, so might other psychologists, so might a jury. They'd better settle. Sometimes lawyers will call me and wisely get a free opinion before they even hire me. I will tell them honestly if they don't have a very good case.

"Will the nine-month-old be traumatized for life if moved from the only home she has ever known?"

"Well, actually, I'm not sure. None of us could be sure of that. I don't believe I can say that."

"Well, then, thank you. Goodbye."

Charmaine's lawyer, Kevin, told me straight up that his client had left her baby for six months in the care of the foster mother whom DCF had found for him. Kevin didn't use the word "abandoned."

She had gone back to Birmingham. She did not call or write. There were telephone appointments with DCF that she missed, which suggested to them that she did not want to know how her baby was doing. But she was now back in Vermont, and her lawyer told me that DCF was not allowing her visits with her son, Benjamin, not even supervised visits.

Charmaine was African American, so I was alert to possible prejudice even though Vermont is known for its liberalism and anti-racism activism despite its overall complexion as one of the whitest states in the US. And what was happening with Charmaine's son, Benjamin, seemed strange. They weren't even letting her see her son at the DCF office, not even for an hour. I've heard of parents who have murdered someone and still have supervised visits with their children. I've seen mothers who left their children alone in an apartment for days with nothing to eat and in one diaper still get supervised visits. This last child was so hungry that when the police found the three-year-old and fed him, he ate three Big Macs. What the hell was happening with Charmaine?

When I spoke to Charmaine, she didn't have the best answer to my questions about why she left and why she didn't check up on her son. She was lively and informative but vague in the way that some people are, people who give lots of information but leave you feeling at a loss to understand them. Her story was that she was trying to earn money back home where she knew she *could* earn money, living with family, because in Vermont she couldn't find a job, and the subsidy for her apartment was about to run out.

She was young, the age of my students who had their entire lives ahead of them. I could imagine her back in the life she led in Birmingham, with family and friends, secure in the fact that her son was being taken care of. She told me she liked the foster mother very much and felt that her son was safe there: "It's a good home."

That kind of made sense to me. If she were a daughter who'd left her son with her own mother, we would understand what she did. But she didn't have a mother to leave her son with. Both her parents were dead. Her sister had children of her own to take care of. Charmaine then came to Vermont, the place she had heard had good benefits for single mothers, a place that would, like a mother, take care of her, a place that would be her othermother.

In the African American community and black diaspora societies, there has been a tradition of othermothers. As the sociologist Patricia Hill Collins has explained, othermothers are an adaptation to oppression, as well as a long-standing practice of women-centered networks of individuals taking on childcare for one another. These othermothers take care of your children, not only because life might make it impossible for you to take care of your children by yourself but also because children need multiple mothers. It's good for them. Around the world, these kinds of caregiving arrangements are the norm. Around the world, siblings become primary caregivers and othermothers. In my attachment evaluations, I value a child's attachment to these othermothers—the aunties, grandmothers, neighbors, teachers, and co-parents. I might refer to them as "collaterals," but I do not dismiss their importance.

I talked to DCF, and they told me they wouldn't allow Charmaine any visits with her son because she kept cancelling phone appointments when she was in Alabama. Their story seemed as vague as hers. They believed she had gotten herself in with some dangerous drug dealers, people she wouldn't have told me about. But why would that lead to no supervised visits in the DCF office?

I could see down this particular DCF road that Charmaine would probably not get her son back. The situation would probably play out in the months ahead, with Charmaine missing visits, having difficulty finding or keeping an apartment, finding or keeping a job, agreeing to see a therapist but not making the appointment, Benjamin getting older all the while and more securely attached to his foster mother. But why deny her a visit? Would this open a legal door they couldn't close? Why not even just one visit? Why not two hours, one hour, one precious hour with her son, holding him, playing on the floor with him once a week? It might feel a little bit strange for this toddler, but he would also surely enjoy this time with this soft, loving, and somewhat familiar woman hugging him, chatting to him, reading him a book, singing a little song.

Charmaine had no othermothers. Not just no othermothers to assist her, but she had no women of color in Vermont to turn to for advice, none with any power or connection to the system. I asked her if she had a black therapist or a black DCF worker, or worked for a black employer, or had a black mentor. I wanted to call up my friends and ask if they had room in their lives for another child who needed a mother. I did ask her if she would give me permission to talk about her plight with a black friend of mine, in order to ask about resources for her. I described my friend Beverly, Bev, director of the Mosaic Center for Students of Color at the very white University of Vermont and an othermother to many of the students of color there. She said yes.

I drove to Bev's, and she and I stomped through the wintery woods behind her home, talking in our usual overlapping style while cracking through ice puddles in Vermont-sensible boots. What could Charmaine do and what could I do for her? Bev already knew othermother history, intellectually and personally. One of her grown sons, the kind of grown son that I have, still a child but grown, still a worry, is being cared for by an othermother. Her tall, handsome boy who stood out on a football field of young white affluent Vermont sons. I would gladly be an othermother to her sons as she would to mine. But our children choose othermothers for themselves.

Sometimes I wish I had sent Willy away in adolescence, to my brother or to one of my best friends to raise him. I wish my parents were alive and they could have taken him for a summer. Any of these othermothers may have interrupted the drug use. These othermothers could have given him the confidence I might have undermined. I would have trusted them to do this. A daughter trusts her mother to do better with her grandchildren than she did with her, and as grandmothers, sometimes they do.

Both of my sons are grown and entrusted to different othermothers, a wife for one and a girlfriend for the other, two women who remind them to take showers, encourage them when they feel down, calm them when they are upset by putting a tender hand on their arm, right below the elbow, to stop them from going too far. I am grateful.

But I am outraged on behalf of Charmaine. Every mother I have seen, whether addicted, mentally ill, developmentally disabled, whether they have left their children, abused their children, allowed their children to be abused, watched their children being abused, all of these mothers have had visits if they wanted them. Who was this DCF worker? I looked her up online and found her. She looked sweet and young. DCF will protect her from my anger if I speak up. DCF is the othermother for this young social worker. But who will be Charmaine's? I wrote to DCF and said that in my expert opinion, they were setting limits too soon and too firmly on visits, and that in my opinion, this most likely had to be a matter of race, of racism.

By writing that letter I risked good relations with DCF, as well as future income. I did so because I had to and because I can take the risk of never getting referrals from them again. In fact, sometimes I just want to give up doing these kinds of evaluations ever again anyway. I don't know why I felt so strongly that I had to take this risk for this particular woman who had undermined her own chances of getting her son back by not making scheduled phone appointments with DCF. That's a big no-no. As a therapist I've often had the feeling that I'm working harder for someone than they are working for themselves. But that's what mothers and othermothers do, frequently, problematically, and, I must admit, sometimes stupidly; that's what we do.

DCF wrote back and said they were not racist. The worker wrote up our conversation for Charmaine's file misrepresenting what I had said. Reading it, I felt, for the first time, like one of the mothers under investigation reading what a DCF worker wrote about me, something that would forever be in a file, something that was wrong. On a phone call with the DCF worker and her supervisor I equivocated, but I had never said there was no harm to a child when a mother leaves for six months without notice. I had said that because Benjamin was still under a year, the harm of that absence would probably be less severe than the harm had he been older. In the end, I heard from Charmaine herself, that she finally got her visits. She did not get her son back, but she got her visits. And once Benjamin was adopted in that good home, with the othermother Charmaine approved of, Charmaine was invited to visit with him often, which she currently does. There was room for all.

8. A FLOCK OF OTHERMOTHERS

I sat in a meeting listening to my colleagues debate the requirements of the doctoral program we had begun the year before. Someone was speaking in paragraphs, defending a point that was inconsequential, and I glanced down at my face-up iPhone. I was waiting to hear if they needed me in court today, to testify by phone in a criminal trial against a man who sexually assaulted Candace, a twelve-year-old girl I had evaluated. The man was her mother's boyfriend. There was a text from attorney Jan Cooper writing to say that they were on break and Candace had been on the stand and was doing very well. I welled up, feeling a deep connection to this girl who had the courage to face the man who had sexually assaulted her and who was telling her story to a judge.

Maybe I also felt a little pleased with myself and relieved that I was right. I had told a flock of othermothers who had huddled around this girl that I thought Candace would do well on the stand, that she could manage it. I told them that I thought it might hurt Candace more if he got away with it and that in the future she might blame herself if she chose not to testify.

Jan was Candace's lawyer. She, the guardian ad litem, the girl's therapist, the high school teacher she had disclosed to, the foster mother, and the DCF worker, all women, had been wrapping themselves around this girl, abandoned by her mother, like those dogs caring for abandoned kittens on YouTube videos. They were a team, discussing after work on the phone what was best for her, worrying among themselves about whether she would freeze on the stand or leave out important aspects of what happened to her and thus not serve her own interests well. They didn't want her to have to see her perpetrator scowling at her from his table in front of the judge, to ever have to face him again. To these othermothers, this abuser was a monster, more terrifying in the single thing they knew about him than perhaps in his actual embodiment. And it would be even worse for Candace to see her mother by his side, not hers.

In Vermont, Rule 807 holds that in a case of sexual assault when a victim is a minor, the attorney, guardian, parents, or guardian ad litem may submit a motion that the child's testimony be taken by two-way closed-circuit television or through a recording. "Only the persons necessary to operate the equipment and a person who is not a potential witness and whose presence the court finds would contribute to the welfare and well-being of the child or mentally ill or mentally retarded person may be present in the room with the child . . ." The accused person's image would be transmitted to the witness, the child sitting in a separate room, unless seeing or hearing the accused person would present a "substantial risk of trauma to the witness which would substantially impair the ability of the witness to testify."

Counseling professionals tend to overprotect victims, especially child victims. There is some potential for what professionals call "retraumatization" when family members don't believe a victim, although "retraumatization" is a bit dramatic a word in my opinion to describe what actually happens. Sure there is sadness and anger when a victim is not believed, but are the effects equivalent to the initial trauma? Worse, as some have even argued? In my opinion, the time in court can exacerbate the symptoms of the original trauma, open doors to old rooms in a haunted castle, but it isn't exactly a reliving of the trauma. It makes fantastic theatre to show a victim on the stand going into a post-traumatic trance when telling her story, but it is much more likely that she will feel uncomfortable and intimidated by the perpetrator and his aggressive lawyer.

When I did my research for this case, calling the "collateral contacts" such as the principal, her teacher, her cousin, her school counselor, and her therapist, I felt an outpouring of love for this girl. These women had banded together, and there was no doubt in anyone's mind that she was telling the truth. Yet each urged me to not recommend that she take the stand and to support the 807 rule. While Candace was a poised twelve-year-old, each argued that her strength was a veneer, an act. I saw it that way, too, at first, but then I also saw that acting as if she were an adult had given her skills and intelligence, emotional restraint, and thoughtfulness. This was a form of strength she'd developed while living in a world where the one being who is supposed to protect you the most has failed you. I wanted to protect her, too, but I wanted her to have this opportunity to say, on the stand, he did this to me, and be believed.

I wrote in my report, after confirming this with Candace, that her greatest fear was not seeing this man in court, the man whom she had lived with for the past three years of her life, the drunk who hit her on the head when she resisted, making her "see stars," as she put it. Her greatest fear was having to see her mother sitting next to him. She hadn't seen her mother since she had disclosed the abuse, and she was afraid of how it would feel to see her mother again, to see her taking her boyfriend's side against her daughter. That would be the kind of hurt that could render a twelve-year-old mute on the stand, that could make her crumble. That was the kind of hurt that would retraumatize her, like the thousand disappointments that likely led to a moment like this. I wanted to convince her advocates that Candace would be all right, because I knew that there was so much more of a likelihood that the boyfriend would be convicted if she testified in court against him.

Jan emailed me to argue against her taking the stand: "But this girl has no mother."

I said to her, "Jan, she has you. You can be there for her. Hold her gaze as she speaks. Be her mother in the courtroom."

And that is how we become the temporary othermothers for those who don't have them, a gathering of women all playing different mother roles, from protector, to nurturer, to holder, to encourager, to mirror. I spoke to all of them.

Years ago I had helped another girl, this one also twelve, take the stand. We had set up a courtroom in the sandbox and acted out what might happen with miniatures. She chose the pig to represent her perpetrator. I helped her to imagine a safe place she could bring to mind while testifying because she was determined to be on that stand and "get him." We worked for weeks on preparation, with deep-breathing exercises paired with imaginal exposure, imagining what it would be like in court. I suggested where she might look when she testified to avoid his eyes. I said I would be there so she could look at me, but when I got to the courthouse, the perpetrator's lawyer had me sit out in the hall on the false grounds that I might be called to testify. This was a ploy to remove support from her when she testified. They removed her mother from the courtroom, too, and we paced the hallway together. Halfway through my client's testimony, there was a break, and the lawyer came out and asked, "What do we do? She's wooden. She's not believable. They think she sounds rehearsed." I didn't know what to tell her and worried that my preparation had undermined what she needed to bring to this moment. But after the break, the defense attorney got his chance. The stupid fellow had her read aloud a birthday card that she had written to her stepfather telling him she loved him. When she read it aloud, she "broke down," weeping so bitterly that three of the jurors started crying too. She explained through heaving breaths that her mother made her write that card, that she wasn't lying. And she was believed. At the sentencing, which I attended, when the click of handcuffs reverberated in the courtroom, I glanced at this little girl who had stood up to her abuser, and her eyes gleamed. She was good. Then she went on with her life and over time, got busy, got the dog she was promised, started going to eighth-grade dances, and didn't come to therapy every week anymore.

Candace took the stand and did well. So many othermothers were there in court that day gazing into her eyes at the crucial moments of her narrative. I hope Candace was proud of herself.

In my department meeting, I was there and not there, my heart bursting with pride for a girl I had only met twice but could imagine solemn and clear on the witness stand. Being there and not there would be a technique that I would have used to help Candace testify if she needed help, but she had already been trained in that strategy. She was a girl who had had to mother herself, a girl who doesn't cry, a girl who is "too adult," but a girl who had the ability to attract so many othermothers to her. They had asked me, "Why should we one more time ask her to be an adult and take care of things?" Because she can, I guess. Because sometimes we miss the strengths in our children that help them to heal themselves—I know I did at times, with my own child. Also, because she is not alone. She has you.

9. A LONG ROAD TO TRAVEL

Al's older daughter has hit the tennis ball over the fence and down the hill into the parking lot for the fifth or sixth time, making her father run for it. She looks delighted to see his friendly trot, like a work dog given a job to do. He's herded the two girls, eight and ten, into the confines of the metal fence around two tennis courts and monitors its edges, chasing balls that go outside. He's athletic for a thirty-six-year-old and handsome, his long blond hair in a ponytail. He's got his messed-up work pants and boots on, but that doesn't interfere with his running to chase the balls both daughters lob glee-fully far and wide. They sparkle in their Disney shirts and shorts that advertise two other sisters who will not be parted, Elsa and Anna. Al asks the eldest, Cassie, to tie her shoe so she won't trip. She is about to resist and give him crap but looks at me, with my notebook in hand, performing my observation, and obeys, smiling.

This father has done most everything that DCF has asked of him. A parenting class. Months working with a Family Time coach during supervised visits. A Batterers Intervention group. He even has a therapist he's stuck with for a couple of years. He is reliable and predictable with his visits. His visits are no longer supervised, and he has had his girls out to his trailer for overnight visits. DCF says when the girls are with him, the children run wild with lack of discipline. He tries to be strict, but DCF says there is no follow-through. A father who no longer is permitted to yell or to threaten to spank may have a hard time otherwise laying down the law.

I see follow-through though. During my observation on the playground, he is using "1, 2, 3" like a pro, sitting his older daughter in a time-out, and giving incentives for good behavior. By the time of this observation on the tennis court, I have already spoken to ten different "contacts" such as foster parents, teachers, and therapists who think that Al is a "good guy." Most also agree he can't organize himself well enough to be a single parent who will be able to get the girls to school on time, with the right clothes, hair and teeth brushed, homework completed.

Gail, the first foster mother, is a collateral contact who described the girls as feral when they first came to her home. Under Gail's care, the sisters were transformed from wolves to little girls, catching up in school, joining sports teams, and cuddling with Gail at bedtime. But they are not with Gail any longer as hers was strictly a foster and not a pre-adoptive home.

This is one reason why I can't make up my mind about these girls: loss. If Al can't show he can care for his daughters, these girls won't have their father. They don't have Gail. And they have lost their mother to addiction. When they were back living with her after a year in foster care, their mother relapsed and died. The little one found her, lying unresponsive on the living room couch. It seems that once an addict has been clean for a while, she can't gauge how much to take, and what got her high before can now kill her.

Can these sisters bear more loss? When they were a family of four, their father beat up their mother and treated her unfairly. During that time DCF barely worked with him, as they focused their support on the girls' mother over a year of trial and error sobriety that ended with the girls' return and then their mother's death. The daughters were then put into another foster home, this time a pre-adoptive home, but DCF also began working hard with Al, throwing him into every group, providing him with every service. There had been a couple of state supreme court cases in Vermont in which a lower court's termination of parental rights had been overthrown because DCF was deemed to have not worked hard enough with a parent or parents. Al was missing work constantly to attend meetings, therapy groups, and parenting classes. And it began to take, even the work he was doing in his batterers' group. He admitted to beating the girls' mother and, perhaps in words he learned in his group, understood it as control: "I tried to control her, but she had a right to the money I earned, and she had a right to go out at night for entertainment. I did." He passed not one but two parenting classes with flying colors.

When I meet alone with the girls, they tell me, "He's changed!" But they remember who he once was too: "I'm still mad at Daddy for hurting Mommy." Mad is good for little girls, to some extent.

We get in our cars to drive from the tennis courts to the "adoptive home," a name that must make Al mad, but he doesn't show it. It says to him that he doesn't have a chance. I follow in my car as Al pulls into a service station parking lot, where a bulked-up black truck waits, parked to the side. Al is not invited on the property of the adoptive home, and so he must transfer the girls to their foster father, Chuck, in this parking lot.

The girls say goodbye to their father and are all over him, the little one swinging from his neck like a chimp, the older one stroking his ponytail. I follow Chuck's truck to the adoptive home that is a child's paradise. There are two big black friendly dogs, both clearly old mutts, on the porch, so relaxed they can't be bothered to come over and take a whiff of the visitors. In the backyard stands a swing set amid statues of gnomes and a pathway of stones leading to a small pond with a fountain. Inside the home the girls share a bedroom with their own TV. The frilly curtains, multiple pillows on each bed, Disney's *Frozen* bedspreads, and hundreds of stuffed animals suggest that here in this home is everything two little girls could ever want, coming as it all does with two loving parents, Jeanine, tall and quiet, and Chuck, a young bundle of father energy.

Jeanine has set a firm boundary between her home and Al, as well as a firm boundary between her home and the girls' last foster home, Gail's. I'm not sure why. Alone with the girls in their bedroom, I ask them to tell me about their last foster home. I am testing them, tweaking their little hearts to see if they are frozen or still beat for those who came before Jeanine. The younger girl's eyes well up. "Do you know Gail? Can we see her?" She begs me because she is sensing where the power lies.

Jeanine, along with DCF, has also set a firm boundary around the last therapist both girls shared, another collateral contact I spoke to, a talkative, playful woman whom the girls were lucky to be able to hold onto for a year. This therapist had spoken well of Dad, but sides had been drawn, and the children had been moved to a new set of therapists whom I have also talked with. They are young and eager, but these wild and challenging little girls have snapped their mouths shut in their offices, guarding against another loss. As I sit with the girls in their Disney bedroom, I ask them about the old therapist they no longer see. Again they both jump at me, "Can we see her again? Can we go back to her?" the younger one stroking my hair.

Girls at ages eight and ten have attachments that are already deep and important. They may be attached to people who are inappropriate, who say the wrong things, who are on the wrong side, people who still pull at their hearts after they have been asked to detach from them. The important thing is that they have attachments. They long for them.

If the court frees these girls for adoption, they may also lose their father. This is the father who beat their mother. But he is their father and, after the death of their mother, they could now also lose him. This thought chills me.

When I am finished for the day, I drive on beautiful country roads at the peak of leaf season. Vast orange mountainsides are turning pale, and a gigantic moon sits low to my left. I pass a famous creamery. I buy their cheese and butter because the workers share in the profits. In that home, there is room for everybody. I see happy trailers, with porches built out from their fronts, with Halloween decorations and pumpkins, and I feel guilty for ever thinking they were ominous sites of abuse.

If we got rid of every father who ever hit his wife, whoever said the wrong thing, whoever kicked or demeaned a child, we'd rid the world of a lot of fathers. My own father would be no good for kids, according to DCF, as he demeaned my mother and shouted all the time. He used to lose his temper daily and throw forks or spoons to the floor in jarring clangs. Maybe my mom made a sarcastic comment over dinner. Maybe a fork was dirty. But he was a good enough father. Didn't all fathers carry on like that? Who knows? I loved him.

Do we normalize male anger? Tolerate it? Understand it? Use it? Admire it? Or are we as women disoriented by it? I know I can't gauge what is an okay amount. I worry when I hear other feminists talk about male aggression; I worry that we exaggerate the impact and power of small expressions of anger because we have experienced the larger ones. Like the continuum of sexual violence where a wolf whistle is at one end of an inevitable track to rape, does every moment of anger stamp a man as a danger? Does it suggest that every man can have a crazy moment when he grabs you by the neck after you call him a creep, holding you there in his grip for just a minute because he can hold you there. He is stronger and you are scared. Would a moment like this inexorably lead to murder, result in trauma? For some women, yes. I guess that's why we can't excuse it.

I saw another man, like Al, who had a history of violence. He was addicted to drugs, drank too much and blacked out, but witnesses report that one night he beat his wife in a particularly horrific way. It was a night when she was high too. The police report shows he hurt her so badly that her face was unrecognizable. She was in the hospital for two weeks. He doesn't remember this night. He is clean and sober now and taking good care of his little girl on the overnight visits he has her. His wife is still using and so has lost visitation, but this man, her abuser, hasn't taken any drugs or drunk any alcohol after that night. I want to believe in his change. So evidently did his wife, as she bailed him out of jail after she got out of the hospital. What over-empathizing, give-em-one-more-chance, he's-hurting-too, see-the-good-in-him women we can be.

My own husband occasionally had fits of temper. And I yelled at him but excused them. I saw them as moments of "emotional dyscontrol" when he got overwhelmed, when his nervous system couldn't take another jibe, or another minute of family chaos. Over twenty-five years, three moments of dyscontrol stand out, as do a few outbursts he was sorry for later. But I wonder if I am also forgetting other times, times I didn't yell back, or times I froze or left the room and went to work at my computer. Do we simply live with male anger as we live in a world where we tolerate meanness, murder, even war?

Nevertheless, I think Paul is good enough. I can give him the honor of being good enough so much more easily than I can give it to myself. I reason that if everyone with a temper couldn't parent, then the foster care system would be overrun with kids traumatized by loss.

Even though my dad lost his temper, a lot, the time that sticks in my memory was when he got so mad he just walked out of the house. Would he come back? A few hours passed, and I worked on homework at the kitchen table with one eye on the front door. He did. He had only walked out of the house to cool off, not to leave us. Loss is so much harder to bear than anger. Anger comes out in a moment, in a scene, then lights out, or curtain, and on to scene two. Loss is forever.

It's dark, and I'm concerned I might not find the house I am looking for. I'm going to meet Paul for dinner with my college friend Andy, who grew up in Vermont on a dairy farm, one of the largest ones once, but when dairy prices fell, subsidies were not enough to keep the barn in good shape. He does okay with a website business. He and his family are the only Vermonters I know who have the Vermont accent. You can't get they-yuh from he-yuh.

Roads are like neural pathways that lead you backwards, or they lead you in the same direction you've always gone, through ruts in the road. Some will lead you nowhere. I've been daydreaming as I drive, about my father, Al, that other father who abused his wife, male violence and female responses to male violence, asking myself if I'm too soft or too understanding. All at once, I ask myself, was I wrong to cut out Willy's biological father from his life? Was this the cause of everything? Am I like Jeanine, the adoptive mother, who wanted to start over? To clean out the past? To set up fences around a childhood paradise? Did I underestimate the importance of the earliest of connections? Or am I once more blaming myself for something I had no power over, because Willy's father left us. My imagined power resides in my decision not to chase him, to forcefully include him, send photos, make financial demands. Like Jeanine, I chose to not work with a messy attachment. I wanted to move on.

As I moved on from my own mother. When did I, a ten-year-old who fell asleep in her mother's bed every night, decide she couldn't rely on her mother anymore, the mother who always seemed too nervous, too easily hurt? Perhaps it was the last time she snuck an insult into a conversation or said to me before I left for an outing, "You're wearing that?" When she exchanged a knowing look with my sister saying I was just like Erica Kane, the selfish beauty from the soap opera *All My Children*.

My earliest memory of our relationship is actually a story I've been told about when I was a baby, a neural pathway nonetheless. When I was born, my mother was afraid to hold me. My father held me. So did the relatives at home who worked with her to help her feel more comfortable as a mother. Auntie othermothers. My grandmother. The story goes that I was so tiny and vulnerable and she felt so incompetent and inexperienced that she was afraid she would hurt me. There have always been others around to help, especially my father, but at a few hours old, I was already too much for my mother to handle.

A few weeks or months after my birth, I'm told I wouldn't stop crying. This is a funny story actually. My mother called my auntie Sugar, named Sugar because she was from the South and would say to us, "Give me sugar," when she wanted a kiss. She had already had three children. She instructed my mother to pick me up, which she did. Then Auntie Sugar told her to walk to the window with me, which she did. Then she told her to open the window. She did. The next instruction was to throw me out. Laughs all around.

But things must have improved to the extent that I needed and could use the comfort my mother provided. I see now my detachment must have started at the end of childhood, developing gradually in adolescence when I chose to be the daughter of a busy, wheeling and dealing father, so proud of me, rather than the companion of a shy, bitter mother (my sister's role). It was also something that made me the best and most loyal friend to my girlfriends because I needed them to see me and find me lovable, which they did.

As a young adult, I jokingly told others that my mother may have loved me but she didn't like me. I went to college and rarely looked back until she got sick. Before she died, I had time with her in which I was able to observe her play with Willy, then two, and a blue parakeet, at her kitchen table. Willy watched the parakeet on my mother's finger as she lifted it to peck a kiss on her mouth. She offered it to Willy's finger and he looked close to bursting with desire to put his fears aside and take the bird on his finger. His eyes intently following the bird, she gently moved the bird back and forth from her finger to his, sensitive to his surprised looks, withdrawing his finger when the jittery bird grasped it. Her words were minimal coos that offered gentle encouragement. I could see she was all a child of two, three, four could want in a mother. She was most likely all that to me once. My father died seven weeks after she died. She had been sick, but his death was unexpected and devastating.

I pull into the driveway between the farmhouse and the fields holding onto now dead crops. My eyes go to the yellow light emanating from the window. A warm harbor after so many Vermont roads. I haven't changed my mind about these girls. They have lost their mother. They cannot lose their father too. I am going to make the best case possible for why the adoptive parents should welcome their father into their lives, into their birthday parties, into their sports games, why at eight and ten they will need both this new family *and* him, because he is not just the man who controlled and beat their mother, but the man who has done the work required of him, a good guy, or rather, good enough—and they are attached.

10. JUDGES

I wasn't able to help Al. The judge went back and forth in his decision too. He also saw the complexity of the case and the impending tragic loss to the girls. But he couldn't settle on the right thing to do. And

I hear from his lawyer that Al gave up trying, which I understand. Those girls were doing well in their foster home. Well enough.

Most of the time I feel as if I collaborate with judges, although we rarely speak directly to one another. They take the burden off me because, in the end, it is their determination that reunites or separates children from their parents. Some judges treat me with solemn respect. Some joke with me. I have learned over the years to look at the judge when I am explaining concepts and not at the lawyer who asked the question. This irritates the lawyer on the other side because he doesn't want me to make a connection with a judge, to create a feeling of camaraderie.

There was none of that with Judge Clarendon, though, who sat high behind the judicial bench. A necklace rested over her black robe's collar. It was a necklace of big wooden blocks in primary shapes and colors, as if to indicate that she liked children, that she would rule on their behalf.

This necklace set me on edge. We're in a court where "If you're happy and you know it clap your hands" is not, in my expert opinion, appropriate. But solemnity is not the overarching climate in court. Judges, security guards, lawyers, and the court reporters often banter. They chit-chat, check in with each other, joke around—and it really makes me uncomfortable. Let's not be happy, even if we know it, because someone else here, often someone sitting at the table in front of us, and listening to the banter, is anxious and about to suffer a terrible loss.

I also dislike when the lawyers seem to enjoy themselves too much during their arguments or objections, when the court process seems fun to them. The parents sitting there must sometimes wonder, What the hell are they laughing about? Don't they realize what's at stake? But sometimes, eerily, the mothers and fathers join in the smiles and laughter, too, everyone colluding in an unreal experience in which both sides are enjoying the competition, forgetting what's at stake. This must be because the child is not at the table. A child would be confused, distraught, among so many cocky adults.

Judge Clarendon ended up being more the schoolmarm than the preschool teacher. She cut me off with a scold and demanded with a sigh that I stop looking down at my report when testifying. She told me I didn't know the law and ruled that I should not deign to make comments about the effects of a child's removal on her foster siblings, or why the federal law recommends that fourteen months in foster care is enough instability for any one child.

In the end, she did not accept my recommendations. She was the first not to do so in the twenty or so years I've been testifying in Vermont, and she tore a three-year-old out of the only home she'd ever known to place her back with her biological parents. I learned about this in a hotel room in Chicago. I was at a conference but wasn't going to any of the talks that day because I had too many papers to grade. I answered my phone, and Dana, the child's lawyer, told me the news. Dumbstruck and instantly guilt-ridden, I said, "I'm so sorry. I wish I had done better for you." Dana reassured me it wasn't me but got off the phone quickly. Maybe she had to get to court or maybe she was crying too.

I filled a bubble-bottomed hotel glass with water and watched my hand tremble. I was terrified for that little girl. I imagined what it would feel like to be her and suddenly lose everything, sister, brother, mother, home, and have to make sense of why she was where she was and why her mother (her foster mother, who in her mind was her real mother) wasn't coming for her. And then I thought about what it would be like to be the foster mother, wanting to save this child but forced into the position of an abandoning mother, unable to undo that impression in the heart of a three-year-old.

The birth mother's lawyer argued that the relationship with the foster mother should be severed quickly and completely because he believed, or pretended to believe, that only in that way could a new attachment be formed with the birth mother. His idea was consistent with those parents who toss kids into the deep end of the pool. His recommendation was sly, and he probably suggested it so that the DCF worker who would be dropping off the child for longer and longer times with her birth parents wouldn't be able to see and document how the child falls apart during each transition and how the birth mother could not soothe a child so bereft.

I stomped all over the hotel room and threw a tantrum in my head saying wild and childish things like, "I hate this judge. I hate her and her stupid necklace." I pictured a scene from a movie where I'd run into her on the steps of the courthouse and rip it off her neck. All the little blocks would scatter on the floor. Close-up shot of blocks on the floor—a symbol of shattered childhood. Cut to crack in blind justice statue.

Anger is protective, as is humor. Both are better than fear, better than empathy. I can't stop thinking of how it will feel for this three-year-old, needing her mother, not being able to have her. We have all felt that, though, haven't we? The desperation when we thought our mother was gone forever? And what did we do then, as children? Perhaps we turned to others. Through force or fate, there were others. Mothers cannot be the whole world. That is too shaky a prospect.

11. PERSISTENCE

Most of the time, when children do lose their mothers, because of my recommendation or another's, I don't know how the lives of the children turn out. I am told the judge's decision by the lawyers or DCF workers, but I rarely hear what happens next, whether the massive system, like neural pathways, has carried them through the next transition with as little harm as possible, whether they even realize there has been a transition, as sometimes their lives change gradually. The Easter Seals Family Time workers no longer come; the visits with their birth parents dwindle; the social worker disappears when the child is officially adopted into the family and settles in. Social workers help the older children with this transition by working with them on memory books. Some adoptive parents give a party marking the adoption day when they go to court and sign the papers. I was invited to one but couldn't go and wanted to preserve the sense in myself that with this celebration for some, there was also a great loss for another woman, a loss I had recommended. Some adoptive parents continue to send letters and arrange visits with birth parents, but this occurs far less frequently than I think would be helpful to children. I understand the urge to wipe out the other mother, the one who lays some strong biological claim on your child in a culture that prioritizes blood ties. This goes both ways, though. If a child is returned to her birth parents, for good, these parents will not make room for the foster mother who loved their child once, whom they've come to see as a cuckoo in their nest.

Some foster mothers are incredible. Fierce. When DCF has failed, when the lawyers are paid, when the judge has moved on to the next case, and when a child is returned to a risky situation, some foster mothers don't quit their mothering.

Vanessa was one of these. She lost Ava, the child she had raised for almost three years. A child she brought home, shortly after birth. This was a child whom her own daughter had come to love. At the home observation, Ava danced for me with her sister and foster brother to the Christmas music playing in the living room, "Giddy-up, giddy-up, giddy-up, it's grand, just holding your hand." Ava collapsed breathing heavily between me and her foster mother on the couch and chatted constantly as precocious little ones can do. Her foster mother reached over to place a large photograph album in front of us, the photos within showing Ava firmly embedded in an extended Vermont family, cousins galore, uncles, aunts, and, I was told, grandparents who love her dearly. "PopPop!" she pointed out happily in response to several photos that showed her foster grandfather among several others in a long line of family at a family reunion. Vanessa told me that Ava and PopPop have a special relationship. I had a twinge of jealousy about this large family, not flung across the US as mine is, a family that has family reunions. Ava had a foster grandfather to dote on her and bring presents and cakes, to read to her.

As tenderly as Vanessa cuddled with Ava, she was as fierce when it came to fighting the system. Trained as a counselor, she had empathy for Ava's birth mother as well as suspicion. She didn't believe that Stephanie, the birth mother, was clean or telling me the truth.

Vanessa reported this to me in a matter-of-fact way and not with any urgency, perhaps because she was used to professionals not believing her or accepting her insights. At first I was suspicious of Vanessa when she emailed me to tell me that Ava fought not to go to visits and said things like, "No like Stephi-Mommy." Some foster mothers who have become attached to their foster children exaggerate. But as visits increased with Stephi-Mommy, Vanessa sent me videos showing Ava not only resisting but coming home from them twirling herself until dizzy and then staring straight ahead, spacing out, dissociating. Over the year of court appearances and increasing visits, Ava grew more clingy and Vanessa more fierce on her behalf.

At recess during the court hearing, Vanessa made a final plea to Stephanie, the birth mother. This happened in private, in a little room off the entryway between the lobby and the courtroom. In this liminal space they didn't need to be enemies. Vanessa promised Stephanie visits, connections, collaboration, and a big welcome into that large family featured in the reunion photos. The lawyers and I paced and chatted in the lobby outside, knowing a tense and important conversation between two mothers could make this nightmare for Ava go away. Stephanie emerged from the room looking confused, saying urgently to Vanessa alone that she wanted to do the right thing for her daughter.

By the next recess, after Vanessa was interrogated on the stand, made to say under oath things about Stephanie she'd rather not have said, the connection made was broken. Stephanie had been in the courtroom and felt betrayed by Vanessa. She resolved to carry on to get her daughter back.

After four days of witnesses, the judge took a few months to write his opinion, and Ava grew older. He made the wrong decision and sent the almost-three-year-old Ava back into the birth parents' home. When DCF asked for my opinion about the best way to proceed with this reunification, I wanted to say, "Don't do it," but I restrained myself and said, "Slowly." There was no way to proceed without trauma.

As visits increased and Vanessa cooperated, we were all scared, dizzy, and dissociated. The lawyers, DCF, and I were mad at ourselves for not being fiercer. But it was Vanessa who was the one who had to pull Ava out of her car seat when she locked her legs against the seats in front of her and who had to pry a clinging child's fingers one by one off of her arms to press her into a car seat in the parents' car for overnight visits. Vanessa learned to stand back over time and let Stephanie do the job she wanted to have, and look on helplessly.

Vanessa was an othermother. One of the othermothers who raise other people's children in our village-less society. It was a blessing that Stephanie's child was placed in such a loving home with music, dancing, books, and family reunions. Therapists are othermothers. Teachers are othermothers. I'm an othermother to a former student of mine, perhaps several. As an othermother, I learned, you don't choose your otherchildren—they choose you. I shine my other-mother eyes on my former students in a different way than I inspect my sons. I am less critical, more appreciative, and more careful to let them form the boundaries of the relationship. I listen, feed them, lend money, receive announcements of engagements, sometimes before their own mothers do. I praise them and give motherly advice that my own sons would be furious to receive.

And I have had othermothers too. I snuck away as a child, down the alley, to spend afternoons with Vivian, a bored housewife who wrote mystery novels and painted. I'd eye the mothers of my friends and boyfriends for potential: Will you be my mother? And in gradu-ate school I got another othermother, one who invited me to her home on the Cape and who took care of Willy when I was in the hos-pital having Julian. These othermothers make us loveable when our own mothers do not. My friends, Sarah and Diane, are othermothers of a kind to me. If my children need othermothers, I hope they find them. I hope these othermothers will do for them what I could not.

There is another othermother in Ava's story. A neighbor who saw Ava with Stephanie and became alarmed at what she saw. This other-mother watched and waited and then, when Vanessa was visiting with Ava at Stephanie's, she surreptitiously passed her a note: "Call me." Later, on the phone, she told Vanessa she had heard Ava screaming from the apartment. She also said she knew that Stephanie was still using drugs. This othermother knew that what she was doing was risky, crossing as she did, that imaginary boundary between your family and someone else's. But when called on by DCF to speak, in what would become a series of interviews and court appearances, she did. She would be threatened and frightened, and have to move, and through all of it hopefully she would remember that what she did was the right thing to do, in the best interests of the child, something in this case I hadn't been able to do.

Vanessa, reenergized by her ally, became alert again and fierce. She went to the director of DCF, who told her what's done is done and the court has given its judgment. She was frantic, making calls, trying to figure out what to do. But even with this flock of other-mothers, none of us could do anything until Ava, three years old, eventually spoke up for herself and asked, at a visit with Stephanie, in front of her foster mother, sister, and brother, as well as the official Family Time coach, "Mommy, why do you hurt me?"

After that moment, everyone went into full throttle action. DCF, lawyers, Vanessa, and Ava's therapist. Ava was moved back to Vanessa's house within a week. And she was back! A different child, an untrusting child, a child who spun to self-soothe and stared straight ahead far more frequently than ever before, but she was a safe child.

She is four now and about to be adopted. She will remain with Vanessa and her brother and her older sister. She will have what we call "attachment issues" and need the mirroring that a bruised and exhausted Vanessa can still provide so well, mirroring that will tell Ava who she is, or even re-create who she is, because young children can't form a self except in relation to another, an other. Winnicott said, "There is no such thing as a baby." He went on to say that if you set out to describe a baby, you will find you are describing a baby and someone else. I am glad that for Ava, that someone will be Vanessa.

12. MY CHILD

Occasionally, when I think of Willy's child, my grandson Charlie, who has severe autism (and I am embarrassed to admit this), I wonder if Willy's drug abuse caused it. I absolutely know the facts and know this can't be so, just as I know that vaccinations do not cause autism. I know that if there were a simple cause of autism, researchers would have discovered this ages ago. But I think like this, because—by now I just recognize this as the way I think. The hyper-responsibility that comes with motherhood. The individual responsibility seeing no other forces, no other mothers or fathers. The narcissism. And maybe I, too, have been influenced, just a tad, growing up with a peasant grand-mother in my home, though I have read that when it comes to illness, we all become peasants again. My grandmother, who fainted when I ran away from home, who once saw a TV show about Hitler and panicked because she thought he had returned, a woman who moved from a shtetl in Poland to Chicago, married, and then worked with her husband in their own delicatessen, never, according to my own mother, having time for her own children—in that East Chicago deli, she prepared stuffed cabbage and matzoh ball soup for the customers while her daughter was left on her own. But later, as a grandmother, as my grandmother, later, when a widow, she devoted herself to her *kinderle*, the grandchildren, and especially to me, her Sharele. I felt only pure and constant love, the kind of love my mother would have liked to have received. My grandmother was my first othermother.

Children get on without the intensive mothering we middle-class mothers aim for, the kind we think produces secure attachment. They get on and find resources within themselves. The story I tell myself about Willy is one in which I continually let him down, one in which I am not a good enough mother. But maybe he didn't need the best mother. Maybe he needed me to be there for him when he was ready to step outside that circle of shame that keeps addicts using and prevents their asking for help. He did ask for help. He came to us and was as honest as he could be, considering. His friends told us that he began the process of trying to quit long before they did. Why were they successful and he not? It wasn't for lack of trying. Some of these questions can't be answered, but that doesn't mean I am to blame.

I used to wish for Willy the life he might have had without the addiction, the life that his friends seem to be having of building careers and taking steps into adulthood in a way their parents can talk about and measure. Milestones. What else do parents discuss?

But he has his own life. And it takes time to get back on track, to get on any track after an addiction. Charlie helps, I think. Because of the autism, Willy can't be a casual father, allowing Eileen to do all the work. He has to think through what his son needs in a very specific way, to help him try to talk, to tickle him to make him smile with eye contact, to encourage him to acknowledge his grandmother when she comes to visit. This he does. A kiss from a two-year-old with autism is more miraculous than a kiss from any other kind of child. There are rewards for Willy with this kind of son, though they are different than the rewards a parent gets from a more neurotypical son. And there are milestones, but not the ones that parents of other more typical children share.

I am sad that Willy may never hear his son call him Daddy, after he was so eager to be a daddy and dreamed, as a child, of being a daddy in a model home in a development of similar new houses, to be a part of a typical American family. And I'm also sad that he and his wife stay away from other parents. Those milestones, the incessant comparing of milestones and accomplishments. Boy, do I know about that.

We wait for Charlie to speak. And we wait for Willy, who is afraid to leave the Suboxone and afraid to give sobriety another try without Suboxone when so much is at stake. Suboxone gave him his life back, and it gave us our son back. So now we wait for him to create those hooks in the world of adulthood that will make a life without drugs solid. When it happens, leaving the Suboxone will be a milestone we will not share with all those other parents. We won't proclaim it on Facebook. But we will celebrate it, while at the same time we continue to wake up in the middle of the night with worry.

I have expectations, even though I know the Al-Anon phrase "Keep your boundaries high, your expectations low, and your heart open." I try not to butt in anymore. When I am sad for him, I try not to panic, and I try to allow him to solve his own problems. Once in a while I throw out some suggestions. If he went back to school, he could be a music teacher in two or three years, with a pension. If he loves photography, and he does have such a great visual sense, why doesn't he set up a studio and a webpage? It's not too late to become an engineer if he really wants to design car dashboards. Graphic design! Sometimes I still think, just as I did when he was younger, that he can do anything.

But I know that this is not the case, and I am pleased for him when he has published an article about the AMG versions of Mercedes-Benz cars. This kind of article shows some brilliance about cars that separates him from everyone else in our family, some engineering mind we observed and tried to nurture as well as we, parents who loved literature and music, could. As a boy he studied *Car and Driver*, and we bought him intricate metal reproductions of real cars, fast cars. See? I tell myself. We nurtured him well.

When I make suggestions to him, I know I am being a fool. But somehow I need to occasionally make them. Willy is finding his own way with his interest in photography, in marketing, in cars, his way out of the ravages of addiction. We are still rooting for him. Just a small encounter with Willy and people do root for him. I can't do more. I can root from the sidelines. But it's his life. It's up to him.

13. GOOD ENOUGH

If attachment becomes the key variable in our understanding of what a child needs, then, as in a Renaissance painting of the Madonna and Child, the world around them recedes to the background, and the viewer will focus on the symbiotic pair in the foreground who represent our fantasy of the perfect if fleeting union of mother and infant. We forget that even the seemingly closed circle of attachment between a mother and a child needs support from the world around them. It is deeply unfair that mothers carry the largest load in what is surely a shared responsibility for children. Motherblame and motherguilt are social mechanisms that relieve everyone else—state, health insurance companies, schools, dads, therapists—from their responsibility. It is just such a complicated issue, the cause and effect of child development, and motherblame is an easy answer.

We focus on attachment, but maybe when we think about the best interests of the child, we ought not to think only about attachment but also loss. I have been a party to tremendous loss. From a child's perspective, almost any child's perspective, neglect is better than loss.

I am soothed by reports down the line that a child is adjusting well, is happy and secure in his or her new home. DCF social workers and lawyers I run into will tell me they have seen these adopted children in school plays, or that the family just came back from a trip to Disneyworld, or that the child is now a straight-A student, or that a mysterious tic has disappeared. And we both, for a moment, feel as if we did good work and that all is well.

But who knows? We are looking at the outsides and not the insides of these children. And we should never minimize the loss they have experienced, some too young to put that loss into words. This loss is captured so well at the end of the film *The Florida Project*, in which a six-year-old girl runs dangerously wild, free, exultant, and so very empowered around a cheap motel where she and her mother live in one room. The hotel manager shoos away child molesters, and her mother's friend who has a job at a Waffle House sneaks the kids breakfast. These are predominantly happy children. We admire in particular the pluck and resourcefulness of Moonee, the leading little girl, seeing she is in danger and judging her mother. This is no way for a child to grow up. Her mother loves her but exposes her to potential dangers on a daily basis. At the end of the movie, before the fantasy flight in the last few minutes, as the social worker and police remove Moonee from her home, this little girl who up until that point has only celebrated life, for the very first time in the film is unhappy. For a moment, the screen is filled with her face as she wails for her mama. She is transformed by loss, necessary and unsavory loss. And we, watching, ask ourselves for a moment whether she really was unsafe, and whether the risk of harm might be less impactful than the grief that will follow?

In spite of what we may hear, DCF fights for families to stay together. If at times they seem to move too quickly towards adoption, it is because often their judgments are based on experience. They see the writing on the wall a bit earlier than less seasoned professionals. If a mother or father lies, doesn't return calls, is not interested in rehab, misses therapy appointments, invites strangers to sleep on her couch, prioritizes her boyfriend over her children, and doesn't make it to her visits, which are only once a week, the DCF worker can predict what comes next but is forced to keep working, trying, hoping. I see the two conflicting points of view they balance—and everything in between. Families need to stay together. Children need permanency.

I have been sick to my stomach more than once in imagining what it will be like for a child to lose her mother. But how long do we give a mother to change her life? And whether or not the addiction is her "fault," the facts remain for many that they are not able to parent while addicted and they are not ready to go through the arduous process of getting clean.

I am an expert witness. To my son's decline because of opiates, but also to his recovery. An expert witness to the health-care, rehab, and insurance systems that fail our children. Expert witness to mothers who try but are judged not good enough, to mothers who are traumatized themselves. I am witness to the agencies that provide psychotherapy but rarely the long-term therapy that provides a mother or a child an othermother to attach to.

Too many of the mothers and fathers I have evaluated have been addicted to opiates. But there is currently a change in the US in our attitude towards drug addiction. As middle-class parents like my husband and me cope with the effects of these drugs on our families, and as we hear about the misrepresentation from makers of the drugs who told doctors they weren't addictive, addicts are less likely to be stigmatized and jailed. In some states, police are given training for getting addicts into treatment rather than arresting them. In some states, people in their twenties carry around the nasal spray Narcan, which is provided free of charge in case, at a concert or party, someone they know needs this drug to reverse an overdose.

But would the mothers I continue to evaluate be good enough mothers if they had never become addicted? When they are high, they leave their children unwatched; they allow strange men to sleep on their couch; they don't provide food or change diapers; they don't use birth control and have second and third children. When high they don't care. Could this have been different if their drugs were legal and prescribed, if Suboxone were available and free, if they had access to therapy that promoted a long-term relationship with an established therapist rather than short-term therapy with the naive interns new to the field who change jobs after a year; if they had the kind of therapy that would hold them and provide the good enough mothering they didn't receive? When I think about the mothers of these mothers and the intergenerational traumas, I'm not sure if drug treatment and therapy are enough.

I know now, from my own experience, not to look at relapse alone in my evaluations, because relapse can be a part of a path to recovery. I will judge these mothers instead on their willingness to access treatment, and how hard they work at it. I will look closely at what the opiates did to their ability to parent and what took them so long to seek treatment. I will see what help they were offered and whether or not they were able to make use of it.

I will still look at attachment and stability and the inner resources of the mothers, those kinds of inner resources that show up on the Rorschach. I will continue to mistrust diagnosis and look at signs of mind-mindedness in the people I evaluate. Can they guess at what their child is thinking? Feeling? Can they do so accurately? Do they care to guess? I will look at the person, addiction aside, and see if what she can provide is good enough.

As an expert witness, I bear witness, but do more than that. Bearing witness is an act of compassion. I also judge, which is not. But maybe it can be. Can a person judge with compassion and understanding for parents who've been through the particular kind of hell of addiction, all the parents who once held their babies in their arms and imagined protecting them from harm, encouraging them in school, loving them unto eternity?

Willy is fine, good enough, more than good enough. He is making good progress building a life for himself in Texas with his wife from France, a country where they don't seem to make the same judgments about addicts that we do, and with their two children, the one with autism who needs Willy to be clean and that is good, and a second one now with such a bright spirit that he will shine his eyes into Willy's for years to come telling him he is loved, he is needed, and that he is a good enough father. I hope he will take that in. I wish him that, if only that, but, if I am truthful with myself, not only that.

Acknowledgments

CLEARLY THE NAMES of everyone except my family members and friends have been changed. I have also changed the names of the lawyers, judges, social workers, other service providers, and Vermont rehab centers. While the stories I tell of their involvement might indicate that I do not trust in their ability to help or heal, that is far from the case. We are compatriots, consorts, collaborators in our work and share the frustration of working with addiction in these times.

I want to thank those who read this work and helped me attempt to write in a different and less academic style. Two writing groups in London took me in and provided me with feedback on various chapters. One, led by Nikk Quentin Woolf, contained the marvelous multi-aged group of writers: Anthony, George, Michelle, Siobhan, as regulars who were both critical and enthusiastic, Michelle often painfully telling me to rid myself of motherguilt, while Nikk patiently suggesting time and again that writing might be the way one does that. The second group of young authors, mostly playwrights, in the Berlin Writers Bloc led by Oliver Michell, were thoughtful readers: Nick, Catherine, Gerard, and others, who showed me that my story as a mother might also have some appeal to people who were much younger than I, as they have struggled themselves with friends and family members with addictions. Frederick Noonan and Richard Fry provided a writing space in London, quiet when I needed it, and company when I didn't. Kevin Koch and his friend Greta Klander checked my memory of Texas witticisms. Lyn Mikel

Brown, so smart, so supportive, always at the ready, gave the book a good read early on and provided the best encouragement around issues of authenticity and moments requiring bravery. Laura Orgel, both a psychologist and my sister-in-law, also read an early draft and advised me on who might be hurt by strong language I needed to temper. Bev simply said that whatever I wrote about her and hers was fine and that she trusts me. An additional group of wonderful friends read the manuscript to provide last minute advice and encouragement—Sharon Horne, Sarah Sappington, Diane Anstadt, and Molly Millwood, whose own book on attachment, marriage, and motherhood is sure to be meaningful to many new mothers.

Most of all, Alex Johnson, who teaches nonfiction writing at Lesley University, provided invaluable and in-depth readings of most chapters in their original and revised forms. She was an incredible guide, helping me to shape the book, knowing when it was important for me to share more or hold back, building my confidence through her emotional responses to the writing. I hope our work together created a lasting friendship. I know she is deeply invested in this project, and her thoughts and kindnesses invisibly touch every chapter.

I'm grateful for having a wise and plain-talking agent, Carol Mann, who has supported my work for years. And grateful for my opportunity to work with an experienced editor, Helene Atwan at Beacon Press, who is caring and so kind, and who brings joy to publishing, even in the contemporary frenzied climate around book promotion. I thank the amazing people at Beacon Press who also have assisted with and taken an interest in this story, who give the impression this book is their project.

Thanks go to the lawyers I spoke with, many of whom gave me unofficial advice, some who read their clients' stories, often no longer recognizable to even them, a couple who gave me official advice. You calmed my fears and showed me the boundaries.

My family supported me. Paul was gracious about every section in which he appeared, reminding me that this was my story to tell, not his, nor the family's. His story might be different and it is his to tell. Julian cared about the book in other ways, wanting to protect the brother he still looks up to. As always, he holds all the complex emotionality of our family and throws it back at us. I hope he will be pleased with the final book. Eileen read the book and in her quiet way approved, which meant the world to me. And Willy. Willy allowed the sadness of those times to reenter his life as he read these words and bravely gave me permission for all of it.

Finally, I thank the parents and children with whom I have worked. I thank in particular the ones whom I was lucky enough to contact and with whom I shared what I had written for their approval. For the others, I have toiled over each and every story to disguise who you are while trying also to highlight moments that shone who you deeply are or were when I met you. I am sorry that what I do has, for some of you, contributed to pain in your lives, and I hope that for those who have their children home with them once again, you are holding them close. I judged you, but I also always judged myself. None of us is ever good enough, so perhaps that makes us all together in this. In the end, whether I blame myself a lot or a little, I still wish I could have held my children closer. Maybe we all do.

Coda

THIS BOOK WAS BASICALLY FINISHED IN 2015. But my younger son, Julian, unexpectedly died on July 6, 2018. So different from Willy, Julian was irrepressible and unstoppable, a pleasure seeker, a chaotic loving mess of a child. Friendship meant everything to him. He never did Oxies or heroin but took part in the drug culture that goes along with following what remains of the Grateful Dead—Phil Lesh, RatDog, and other tribute bands—attending music festivals all over the states and club shows in Brooklyn. He smoked weed. He talked up the benefits of LSD but swore it had been a while since he dropped acid. A stupid combination of drugs that would help him sleep after an extended Fourth of July get-together did him in. I haven't changed the parts of this book that describe him as he was at the time of writing, when he was alive. My story as a mother, Willy's story, remains the same. But now, in my life, in my family's life, everything has changed. Irreversibly. Unfathomably. I keep thinking of the line from a Grateful Dead song, "If the thunder don't get ya, the lightning will." My story about mothering the wild, goofy, and loveable Julian is a different one from the story of mothering Willy, still full of worry and, of course, self-doubt, but not necessarily about being "good enough." I hope to write that story someday.

—SL
August 2018